Eustace Alfred Reynolds-Ball

Cairo of Today

A Practical Guide to Cairo and its Environs

Eustace Alfred Reynolds-Ball

Cairo of Today
A Practical Guide to Cairo and its Environs

ISBN/EAN: 9783337177935

Printed in Europe, USA, Canada, Australia, Japan

Cover: Foto ©Andreas Hilbeck / pixelio.de

CAIRO OF TO-DAY:

A PRACTICAL GUIDE TO CAIRO AND ITS ENVIRONS

BY

E. A. REYNOLDS-BALL, B.A., F.R.G.S.

AUTHOR OF 'MEDITERRANEAN WINTER RESORTS,'
'THE CITY OF THE CALIPHS,' ETC.

WITH MAPS AND PLAN OF CAIRO

LONDON
ADAM AND CHARLES BLACK
1898

CONTENTS

PART III.—THE NILE AND ITS MONUMENTS

PART IV.—POLITICAL AND ANTIQUARIAN

MAPS

INTRODUCTION

Cairo, in spite of the Europeanising tendencies of Mehemet Ali, and the innovations of Ismail in his attempt to give a Parisian veneer to his oriental Capital, still remains one of the most attractive cities in the East. It is, of course, inferior in world-wide interest to Jerusalem or even Rome or Athens, but if a plebiscite were taken among tourists of the dozen most interesting cities in the world, Cairo would undoubtedly find a place in the list.

Cairo, dating only from the tenth century, has of course no pretension to rank as an ancient historic capital, and its historic interest is purely Mediæval and Saracenic. In short, the capital of Egypt, the cradle of the oldest civilization in the world and the fountain of European arts and sciences, is but a city of yesterday compared to Memphis, Heliopolis, Thebes, and other ancient cities of Egypt now buried under the desert sands, or the accumulation of the debris and rubbish of centuries.

But though historical students and erudite Egyptologists may consider Cairo a mere mushroom city, it is full of attractions for many tourists, who do not find it easy to resist the fascination of the picturesque oriental life in the native quarters. Fortunately the 'Haussmannizing' of the Khedive Ismail's builders was mainly confined to the European quarter of the city, and did not touch the region of the Bazaars, where it is still possible, when once the Mooski—no longer a purely oriental highway—is crossed, for the imaginative traveller to realise the dreams of the Arabian Nights of his childhood. The artist, too, if he strikes out a line for himself, and ignores the hackneyed and limited itineraries of the interpreters and guides, will find Cairo full of the richest material for his sketch-book.

Some portions of the chapters in *Cairo of To-Day* are reproduced by permission from my monograph, *The City of the Caliphs* (1 vol. 12s. 6d. nett), recently published by Messrs. Estes and Lauriat, Boston, Mass. I have also quoted largely from articles contributed to the *North American Review*, the *Queen*, and other periodicals.

PART I

CAIRO

I.—HOW TO REACH CAIRO

THE number and variety of routes is a little bewildering. They may most conveniently be divided into sea and overland routes. On the whole the voyage is preferable for invalids to the rail journey, and in the long run it will be found, even by the more expensive Peninsular & Oriental and Orient liners, more economical.

(1) Sea Routes.—(1) *From London.*—From London there is the weekly P. and O. service and the fortnightly service of the Orient liners. The P. and O. steamers leave Tilbury every Friday, arriving at Port Said about twelve days later. Fares, London to Cairo (*viâ* Port Said, thence by rail) £21 : 14s. first, £12 : 7s. second.

Hitherto the P. and O. Company have rather neglected the Egyptian passenger service, but during the coming season (1897-98) a new Egyptian service has been established experimentally from London to Alexandria *viâ* Marseilles, leaving London November 25th and December 9th, and afterwards fortnightly, and arriving at Alexandria on December 8th and 22nd. Passengers will be transferred at Marseilles (see page 9) to the S.S. *Clyde* (transferred from the Venice-Alexandria to the Marseilles-Alexandria line), calling at Malta *en route*. Fares, London to Alexandria, £20 first and £12 second saloon. Return tickets have lately been discontinued between London and Egypt (except on Venice line), but a rebatement of 33% on the return passage money will be allowed within four months of arrival. This new service can be recommended to invalid travellers.

The Orient liners sail from Tilbury on November 26th,[1] and fortnightly thereafter, and reach Port Said (calling at Naples) in twelve or thirteen days. During the Egyptian season they also call at Marseilles. First-class fare, London to Cairo (*viâ* Ismailia) £20 : 14s., and return (available for four months) £33 : 8s.

Then the British India Co. despatch one of their steamers on November 26th, and fortnightly thereafter, and take passengers for Egypt, but these steamers are slow, and the accommodation is less luxurious than that provided by the P. and O. and Orient ships. First-class fare to Port Said, £17.

(2) *From Southampton.*—The monthly Australian service of the North German Lloyd Company is coming into favour with English travellers. A

[1] All dates apply only to the Season 1897-98.

steamer of this line leaves Southampton on December 6th, and fortnightly thereafter. The fares from London to Cairo are moderate: £19 : 1 : 6 first and £11 : 3 : 6 second.

(3) *From Liverpool.*—There are numerous steamship services from Liverpool, sailing every fortnight or three weeks, and taking passengers for Port Said or Ismailia. They include the following lines:—Clan, City, Bibby, Hall (not to be confused with Messrs. Hall's steamers to the south of Spain), Anchor, and Glen. The best are the Bibby and City lines, which provide good accommodation at reasonable rates.

The Bibby (a comparatively new company) is a very fast line, and is becoming very popular with Anglo-Indians. Only saloon passengers are taken, and a surgeon is carried. They sail from Liverpool on December 1st and 22nd, and about fortnightly thereafter. Saloon fare to Port Said, £17.

The Anchor Line is cheaper, the saloon fare to Port Said being only £12 (return £21 : 12s.). Sailings on December 2nd and 24th, and afterwards fortnightly. First-class return (six months) to Cairo (*viâ* Ismailia), £25 : 2 : 6.

The City steamers all carry a surgeon, and no second-class passengers are taken. Sailings about fortnightly from December 4th.

The rates of the other steamship companies to Port Said vary from £11 to £15 : 15s. The voyage occupies from fourteen to fifteen days usually. The above services are useful for tourists who wish to travel economically, but, with the exception of the Bibby, City, and Anchor, they cannot be unreservedly recommended to ladies or persons in delicate health.

(4) *From Manchester.*—A new passenger service to Egypt and the Holy Land, known as the Prince Line, has recently been started. Each vessel is 3000 tons burthen, and is lighted with electricity. Doctor carried. Sailings every three weeks from November 20th, calling at Gibraltar, Tunis, Malta and Alexandria. First-class fares from Manchester or London to Alexandria, £13 single and £24 return (ticket available for six months).

There are also the Moss and Papayanni steamers, but these are small, and passengers would probably find a second-class berth on the P. and O. or Orient boats preferable to a first-class one on these vessels, which are mainly intended for freight. They offer, however, one advantage, for, calling at Alexandria instead of Port Said, there is a much more comfortable railway journey to Cairo. Fares by both lines £14 single and £24 return, first class.

Those travelling by the Indian liners are recommended to leave the ship at Port Said instead of Ismailia, and make use of the light railway which has recently been constructed between that port and Ismailia. By this means time is saved, and the discomfort of coaling at Port Said is avoided. Trains leave Port Said at 9 A.M. and 3.42 P.M., connecting with the Egyptian Government trains at Ismailia, which reach Cairo at 5.5 P.M. and 10.35 P.M. respectively.

(2) Overland Routes.—The principal continental routes, classified according to port of embarkation, are as follows :—

(1) *Brindisi.*—This is the shortest and most popular, and the one taken by the mails. The route is *viâ* Calais, Paris, Turin, and Bologna. The P. and O. mail steamer leaves Brindisi for Port Said on Sunday evening as soon as the mails are on board, arriving on Wednesday evening or Thursday morning. In order to catch this steamer passengers must leave London by the Thursday evening continental mail. The fares are £11 : 18 : 11 first and £8 : 5 : 5 second class *viâ* the Mt. Cenis route, and £12 : 2 : 8 and £8 : 10 : 3 *viâ* the St. Gothard. The extra charge for a berth in the sleeping car from Paris to Turin is £1 : 3 : 6, and from Paris to Milan, £1 : 10 : 3. Luggage by these ordinary trains cannot be registered to Brindisi, but only to Modane or Chiasso. The

rates are :—Between London and Modane, 6s. for every 20 lb. over 56 lb.; between Modane and Brindisi, 4s. 4d. for every 20 lb. of luggage.

Those who do not mind expense can take the special P. and O. Brindisi express, with restaurant and sleeping cars attached, which leaves Victoria and Charing Cross at 9 P.M. on Friday, arriving at Brindisi at 5.35 P.M. on Sunday, thus shortening the journey by over twelve hours. Fare: first-class, and for P. and O. passengers only, £16 : 16 : 6. Accommodation being limited, application for places must be made at the P. and O. Company's office, 122 Leadenhall Street, or at the Sleeping Car Company's office, 14 Cockspur Street, S.W. By this service luggage can be registered from London to Brindisi, and is *not examined* either by the French or Italian Customs. The fare from Brindisi to Port Said and Ismailia is £10 first and £6 second. From Port Said or Ismailia passengers can go on to Cairo by rail. Excess luggage is heavily charged for, and the usual plan is to send heavy baggage by goods train. A good deal more luggage can, however, be taken in the carriage with the passenger than on continental railways. A tip to the guard will generally facilitate this.

By the new seven years contract of the P. and O. Company with the English Government, which comes into effect in February 1898, the voyage to Egypt will be accelerated, as the contract time for the mails from Brindisi to Bombay is to be reduced to fourteen days. With this view the company is building two fast vessels, the *Isis* and the *Osiris*, which will run from Brindisi to Port Said in forty-eight hours, being sixteen hours less time than the present service. By this means the communication between London and Cairo will be effected in less than *four days and a half*.

The Austrian Lloyd's mail steamer leaves Brindisi for Alexandria direct every Thursday at 2 P.M. in connection with the express leaving London (Victoria) at 9.5 P.M. on Monday. Fares, 83.50 florins first, and 56.70 florins second class. This steamer runs in connection with the new Ostend-Trieste express (see *Train de Luxe Services*).

Then there is the service of the Navigazione Generale Italiana, leaving Brindisi for Alexandria direct every Friday at 2 A.M. Fares, 171 fr. first, and 118 fr. second class.

(2) *Venice.*—The P. and O. Company run, under contract with the Italian Government, a regular service between Venice, Brindisi, and Egypt, connecting at Port Said with the steamers to India, Australia, etc., while during the winter the steamers sail from Brindisi direct to Alexandria, leaving

Brindisi December 9th, 30th, and afterwards every three weeks.

The S.S. *Sutlej* (4164) has taken the place of the S.S. *Clyde* (transferred to the Marseilles-Alexandria service) for this Venice-Alexandria service. Sailings from Venice (arriving at Brindisi two days later) every three weeks from December 8th. First-class fares to Port Said or Alexandria £12, and £8 second. From London the direct route is *viâ* Calais, Basle, and the St. Gothard. Fares, £8 : 8 : 1 first, and £5 : 18s. second. Time 41 hours. Through carriage Calais to Milan. Sleeping car, Calais to Bâle, 16s. 6d.; Milan to Venice, 10 fr.

Then, every other Tuesday morning at 6 A.M. one of the steamers of the Navigazione Generale Italiana (Florio-Rubattino) leaves for Alexandria. These boats, however, though well manned and well found, are not altogether suited to English passengers, as the hours of meals—10.30 A.M. lunch (or breakfast) and 5.30 P.M. dinner — are not in accordance with English tastes.

(3) *Naples.*—The P. and O. Company have recently discontinued calling at Naples, but there is the weekly service of the Navigazione Generale Italiana, leaving every Wednesday at 5 P.M. for Alexandria direct, arriving on Monday morning. The quickest route from London to Naples is *viâ* Calais, Turin,

and Rome (50½ hours). Fares, £11 : 0 : 8 first, and £7 : 12 : 8 second. Sleeping car, Paris to Rome, £2 : 0 : 2. There is also the Orient Company's service already referred to, leaving Naples at midnight on 5th December, and fortnightly thereafter. Fares to Port Said, £10 first and £6 second class. The North German Lloyd's fares to Port Said are the same. Sailings fortnightly from 15th December.

(4) *Marseilles.*—This port is rapidly becoming a favourite place of embarkation for passengers to Egypt. There are two excellent services to Alexandria by the new service of the P. and O. Company (already referred to) and that of the Bibby line, The Peninsular and Oriental boats sail on December 3rd, and thenceforward every other Friday at noon. The vessels call at Malta, and arrive at Alexandria in five days after leaving Marseilles, thus the whole journey from London to Egypt can be managed in six days and a half. Fares, £13 first and £9 second.

A special sleeping-car service in connection with this Marseilles-Alexandria service, leaving Calais for Marseilles (in connection with the 11 A.M. express from Victoria and Charing Cross), has been established for the season 1897-98. It leaves every alternate Wednesday from December 1st. The train runs alongside the quay. Fare, from London, £9 : 9 : 8. Luggage can be registered through to Marseilles.

The fast mail steamers of the new Bibby line, which call regularly at Marseilles *en route* to Colombo and Rangoon, leave that port for Port Said on December 8th and 29th, and afterwards about every three weeks. First-class fare £12, and £21 : 10s. return. By this service Cairo is reached in seven days from London.

The Messageries Maritimes steamers leave Marseilles for Alexandria direct every Thursday at 4 P.M., arriving on Tuesday morning. Then their Australian and Mauritius steamers call four times a month at Port Said. Fares, 400 fr. first and 300 fr. second class.

(5) *Genoa.*—There is the fortnightly service of the Navigazione Generale Italiana every second Saturday at 9 P.M. from 4th December for Alexandria (voyage seven to eight days). Then fortnightly from 14th December, a steamer of the North German Lloyd sails for Port Said, calling at Naples. (See Naples routes.)

Train de Luxe Services.—By the Orient Express, leaving Charing Cross and Victoria every Sunday at 10 A.M., Constantinople is reached at 1.50 P.M. on Wednesday in time to catch the Khedivieh steamer (leaving at 3 P.M.), which was intended to arrive at Alexandria on Friday evening. Thus, if time were kept on the steamer, Egypt would be *reached in five and a half days* from London. But this promise was not kept, owing to political disturbances and the Greco-Turkish War, and Alexandria was seldom reached before Saturday morning. During the season 1897-98 it is expected that the steamer will arrive at Alexandria on Friday evening. Fare, London to Cairo, £26 : 14 : 3; Constantinople to Alexandria, £7 : 3 : 7 first class. The comparative failure of this Egyptian portion of the Orient Express service probably brought about the new direct weekly service *de luxe viâ* Ostend and Trieste, which was commenced in September 1897. This leaves Charing Cross or Victoria at 10 A.M. on Monday, and there is no change of carriage between Ostend and Trieste, which is reached at 9 o'clock on Wednesday morning. The Austrian Lloyd steamer leaves at noon, and Alexandria is reached early on Sunday morning, and Cairo at 12.50 P.M. Fare, London to Cairo, £25 : 16 : 9.

Then there is the new *train de luxe* service from London to Marseilles in connection with the P. and O. Co.'s new Alexandria service. One great advantage is that luggage is booked through to the steamer and *not examined at all* by the French Customs. Only P. and O. passengers can travel by this train. Fare, £2 : 15s., in addition to ordinary first-class fare (£6 : 14 : 8).

BANKS.—Imperial Ottoman Bank, Sharia (Street) el-Maghraby; Bank of Egypt, Sharia Kasr-en-Nil; Anglo-Egyptian Bank, Sharia Kasr-en-Nil; Credit Lyonnais, near the Post-Office; Thos. Cook and Son (Egypt), Limited, Shepheard's Hotel; Henry Gaze and Sons, Limited, 7 Rue Khamil Pasha.

Baths.—Hammam Schneider, near Shepheard's Hotel. Swimming bath, 5 piastres; Turkish bath, 16 piastres. Open from 7 to 10 A.M. for gentlemen, and 10 A.M. to noon for ladies.

Cafés and Restaurants.—There are several good *cafés* and *cafés chantants*, such as Café Egyptien, close to Shepheard's, the Eldorado, Rue Esbekiyeh (native dancing girls). The best are in the Esbekiyeh Gardens. Usual charge for a cup of coffee or glass of lager beer is two piastres. Santini's, in the Esbekiyeh Gardens, is the best restaurant. Dinners sent out. St. James's Grill Room in the Sharia-el-Maghraby; Grill Rooms also at Shepheard's and

Continental Hotels. Luncheon bars at the Savoy Buffet, New Bar and Sphinx, all in the Esbekiyeh quarter. At these Allsopp's and Bass's ale and American drinks can be had. French billiard room at most of these establishments. Charges: day 4 p., and night 6 p. per hour.

Chemists.—New English Dispensary, Place de l'Opéra (English diploma); English and German Dispensary, near Paschal's, Rue de l'Esbekiyeh; Anglo-American Pharmacy, Place de l'Opéra; London Pharmacy (Myrialaki), near the New Hotel; Agent for Bayley and Co.'s Perfumery and Toilet Soaps.

English Churches.—All Saints, near the Hotel d'Angleterre; chaplain, Very Rev. Dean Butcher. Sunday services, 6.30 A.M., 10.30 A.M., and 6 P.M. St. Mary's, opposite the Bank of Egypt; same hours of service. There are also a Presbyterian Church and two Roman Catholic Churches.

Clubs.—Turf Club, Sharia-el-Maghraby; Khedivial Club, 22 Sharia-el-Manakh; Khedivial Sporting Club (or Ghezireh), Sharia-el-Madabera; Cycling Club, facing the Ismailia Canal.

Conveyances—Cabs.—By the course (within the walls) 4 p. By time, 6 p. an hour or less. Over one hour, 1 p. each quarter of an hour. Each article of luggage carried outside, 1 p. *N.B.*—These official tariffs are practically a dead letter among English visitors, and must be considered as approximate only. The tariff for the whole day is 60 p.

There is a special tariff for the following drives :—

	Single.	Return.	
Polo Ground (Ghezireh)	5 P.	15 P.	1 hour's wait allowed.
Abbassieh Barracks	7 "	15 "	1 " "
Citadel . . .	7 "	15 "	1 " "
Ghezireh Race-Stand (race days) . .	10 "	30 "	3 " "
Tombs of the Caliphs	10 "	30 "	3 " "
Museum . . .	10 "	20 "	2 " "
Heliopolis . .	20 "	40 "	2 " "
Pyramids . .	50 "	77 "	3 " "

Bargaining is, however, advisable, as the Cairo cab-driver will occasionally take less, especially if the visitor speaks Arabic.

Donkeys.—A good way of getting about the native quarters of Cairo is to hire a donkey by the hour (3 or 4 piastres), or by the day (10 to 12 p.), using the donkey-boy as a guide. These donkey-boys are one of the recognised institutions of Cairo. They are a smart and intelligent set of lads, and, as a rule, very obliging and communicative. They have a playful habit of christening their donkeys with the names of English celebrities, both male and female—a somewhat equivocal compliment.

Electric Tramway.—Four lines have now been opened: from the Citadel to the Railway Station;

Citadel to Boulaq; Railway Station to Abbassieh; Esbekiyeh to the Khalig (opposite Roda Island). Fares for the whole distance, 1 p. first, and 8 mill. second class, with a minimum charge of 6 and 4 mill. respectively. A line is being constructed to the Ghizeh Museum and the Pyramids.

Saddle-horses.—The usual charge is 30 p. the half day and 50 p. the whole day.

Carriages.—Victorias and dog-carts can be hired at the Cairo office of the Mena House Hotel, or at Shepheard's or the Continental. The usual charge is 50 p. for the morning or afternoon, and 80 p. for the whole day. Ladies' saddles can be had for 4 p. a day or 20 p. a week.

Cycles.—These can be hired of Messrs. Moring and Co., near Continental Hotel; Baiocchi (gunsmith); A. Joubert, Avenue de Boulaq; and at the Cycling Club.

Dahabeahs can be hired from Messrs. Cook or Gaze. The former firm have a large fleet of modern dahabeahs and a steam one.

English Dentists.—Waller Bey, Mooski; Mr. C. F. Faber (American), opposite Shepheard's.

English Doctors.—H. P. Keating, M.B., 60 Sharia Masr-el-Atika; H. M. N. Milton, M.B., Sharia Kasr-en-Nil; A. A. W. Murison, M.D., Sharia Kasr-en-Nil; F. M. Sandwith, M.D., Sharia-el-Maghraby; K.

Scott, M.B. (oculist); W. H. Wilson, M.B., Pension Tewfik.

Dragoman for the Nile Trip.—Best to apply to the hotel manager or Messrs. Cook or Gaze. In Murray's Guide a useful list of well-recommended dragomans is given. For ordinary guides, or *valets-de-place,* 30 to 40 p. a day is the usual charge.

English Stores.—Messrs. Walker and Co., near Royal Hotel; Mortimer and Co., 24 Sharia-el-Maghraby; Fleurent, opposite Credit Lyonnais.

Forwarding Agents.—H. C. Crozier (agent for Pitt and Scott), opposite Shepheard's; Large and Co., opposite Shepheard's.

House Agents.—Congdon and Co., Sharia Kasr-en-Nil.

Language.—English, French, and Italian are understood in the principal hotels and shops. The donkey-boys, too, can generally add a fair smattering of English to their other accomplishments. Tourists and sportsmen intending to travel in the interior are recommended to learn a few ordinary phrases in Arabic, or they will be absolutely dependent on their dragoman. A few Arabic phrases likely to prove useful, selected from a list published in Mr. Bensilum's useful *vade mecum, The Little Treasure,* published annually in Cairo (price 3 p.), are given below.

Carriage, *Arabeah.* By the hour, *Bil Saah.* By distance, *Towseela.* Get me a donkey, *Geeb homar.* What do I owe you? *Kham lak andee?* I don't speak Arabic, *Ma arafshi arabee.* Can you speak English? *Tet kallam Inglese?* Go on, *Rooah.* Go slower (to cabman), *Bish wesh.* Straight on, *Doogree.* Yes, *Aywa.* No, *Là* (also *Mafeesh*). Go faster (to cabman), *Bil agal.* Go to the Moosky, *Rooah fil Moosky.* To-morrow, *Bookra.* To-day, *Enaharda.* Never mind, *Maalésh.* Get away! Be off! (to beggars and shoeblacks) *Imshee!* Come here, *Taala hena.* It is too dear, *Ghalee Keteer.* Good-day, *Naharak saieed.* What time is it? *El saa kham?* It is one o'clock, *El saa wahdah.* What place is this? *Ay el mahâll dà?*

Living Expenses.—As might be supposed from the hotel charges, Cairo is not a cheap place to winter at. Provisions and necessaries are rather dear, and curiosities, bric-à-brac, etc., extremely so, if time is not taken to bargain for them. The rents of villas and apartments are very high, and even a bed and sitting-room (in the European quarter) would cost from £7 to £8 a month.

Money.—French and English gold is usually accepted at the principal hotels and shops, but the legal currency is confined to Egyptian coins. The unit is the piastre (10 milliemes), which is worth 2½d., and 100 piastres are equal to one Egyptian sovereign, but in official accounts only Egyptian sovereigns and milliemes are reckoned, piastres being ignored. An English sovereign is usually reckoned as 97½ piastres, and the usual rate of exchange for a French louis is 76½ to 77 piastres. The Egyptian coins most in use are 50 and 100 piastres (Egyptian sovereign) in gold; 10, 5, 2 and 1 piastre in silver, and 1, 2, and 5 milliemes in nickel; and there are also copper coins of ¼ and ½ millieme (usually obtainable only at the money-changers), which will be found useful in dealing with the innumerable beggars of Cairo. English sovereigns are universally accepted at the rate of 25 fr., but francs are sometimes refused. "The difficulty of calculation in this coinage is increased by the fact of popular reckoning by piastres being at *current value*, usually half the tariff standard; in a bazaar one is asked 20 piastres when 10 of legal coinage is really meant" (*Where to Go Abroad*, A. and C. Black).

Newspapers.—An English society weekly, called the *Sphinx*, was started in 1893. The *Egyptian Gazette*, published daily at Alexandria, is however the only real English newspaper published in Egypt—Editor and Proprietor, Mr. Andrew Philip. The official Government organ (French and Arabic) is published three times a week. There is a French daily, called *Le Journal Egyptien*—Principal Editor, M. Emile Barrière Bey.

Nursing Fund for Private Nurses.—Hon. Sec., Dr. F. M. Sandwith.

English Nursing Home.—Near the Hotel Continental — Directress, Miss James. The Victoria Hospital is a paying hospital. Hon. Sec., Dr. Murison.

Official Directory—

The Khedive, His Highness Abbas Hilmi II.

English Minister-Plenipotentiary, Lord Cromer, G.C.B., British Agency, Kasr-el-Dobara.

English Members of the Government:—

Adviser on Internal Affairs, J. L. Gorst; Financial Adviser, Sir Elwin Palmer, K.C.B., K.C.M.G.; Judicial Adviser, Sir John Scott, K.C.M.G.; Director of Public Works Department, Sir J. E. Garstin, K.C.M.G.

British Consul, Raphael Borg, C.M.G., 14 Sharia-el-Maghraby.

General commanding Army of Occupation, Major-General Sir Francis W. Grenfell, G.C.M.G., Sharia Kasr-en-Nil.

Sirdar of the Egyptian Army, Sir Herbert H. Kitchener, K.C.B., K.C.M.G.

U.S. Consul-General, Mr. T. S. Harrison.

U.S. Vice-Consul-General, Mr. E. Watts.

Passports.—These are no longer necessary for travelling in Egypt, but foreigners making a long stay are expected to register themselves at their respective Consulates.

Postal Arrangements.—The principal Post Office is in the Esbekiyeh Square. Open from 7 A.M. to 6 P.M. (later on days of arrival of foreign mails). Branch offices at Shepheard's and Ghezireh Palace Hotels. Cairo is six days from London by post. Letters 2½d. the ½ oz.

Mails to and from England

OUTWARD

Day of Departure From Cairo.	*Latest hour at P.O.*	*Route.*
Fridays . . .	9.0 A.M. .	Marseilles.
Saturdays . .	9.0 „ .	Brindisi (Austrian).
Wednesdays . .	10.30 P.M. .	Naples.
Sundays and Tuesdays (uncertain) . .	Uncertain .	Brindisi (English).

INWARD

From London.	*Due in Cairo.*	*Route.*
Wednesdays .	Tuesdays .	Marseilles (irregular).
Fridays . .	Thursdays .	Brindisi.
Sundays . .	Saturdays .	Constantinople (irregular).
Mondays . .	Sundays .	Brindisi.
Mondays . .	Sundays .	Naples.

Parcels.—Under 2 lbs. 1s. 3d.; over, 7½d. per lb. up to 11 lbs. They are made up in London for despatch by the P. and O. steamers every Wednesday. If *viâ* Brindisi, under 3 lbs. 2s. 6d. Usual time of transit, 13 to 17 days.

Telegrams.—To England from Cairo, 1s. 10d.; from Alexandria, 1s. 7d. a word. Local telegrams cost 2 piastres for eight words. Head office, Sharia-el-Boulak. The foreign telegraph office is at 15 Sharia-el-Manakh.

Railway Stations.—Central Station, beyond the Ismalia Canal, close to the Cairo end of the Shubra Avenue; station for Abbassieh, near the Central Station, but on the opposite side of the Canal; station for Helouan, Bab-el-Luk Square.

Reading Rooms and Circulating Library.—Diemer's Library, Shepheard's Hotel Buildings.

English Sanitary Engineers.—Mr. John Price; Mr. W. Hamilton, Kasr-en-Nil.

Shops.—The following are a few of the principal shops which can be recommended to visitors :—

Booksellers.—Diemer, Shepheard's Hotel Buildings; Barbier, Sharia-el-Manakh; C. Livadas, opposite Shepheard's Hotel; Zacharia, opposite Shepheard's; Penasson, adjoining Credit Lyonnais.

Bootmakers.—Calligopoulos, next Cook's office; Karmann Brothers, entrance of the Mooski.

Cigarette Manufacturers.—H. and G. Flick, New Hotel Buildings; Dimitrino, opposite Shepheard's; Ed. Laurens, opposite Splendid Bar; N. Giannaclis, Mooski; Kyriazi Frères, Mooski; D. A. Marusopulo, Rue Kamel, Esbekiyeh.

Cigar Importer.—H. and G. Flick.

Confectioners.—Gyss, Place de l'Opéra; Mathieu, Esbekiyeh.

English Drapers.—Davies, Bryan and Co., New Hotel Buildings; Mrs. Cole, London House, opposite the Opera House.

Dressmakers. — Mme. Cécile, Credit Lyonnais, Esbekiyeh; Miss Roberts, opposite Shepheard's; Mrs. Farrow, Sharia-el-Manakh. Mme. Hoüel, Sharia Abd-el-Aziz.

Florists.—Eggert, next Cook's Offices.

Glovers.—Paschal and Co., Rue Esbekiyeh.

Gunsmith.—M. Baiocchi, Exchange Square, opposite the Ottoman Bank.

Hairdressers.—S. Legana, New Hotel Buildings; De Luca; Ilacqua, both opposite Shepheard's.

Ladies' Hairdresser and Masseuse.—Mme. Schauper, 24 Kantaret-el-Dikkah.

Hatter.—Boni, Place de l'Opéra.

Livery Stables.—Bonnici (saddle horses), behind Shepheard's Hotel; Amato, near Victoria Hospital; A. Ferrari, veterinary surgeon.

Milliners.—Mme. Aug. Pétot and Co., Esbekiyeh.

Oriental Wares.—Malluk and Co. (carpets), Place du Mooski; J. Parvis (bronzes and mushrabiyeh); Cohen, Khan Khalil (rugs and carpets); E. Hatoun, Mooski.

Outfitters.— Davies, Bryan and Co., New Hotel Buildings; Paschal and Co., Rue Esbekiyeh; Mrs. Cole, London House.

Photographers.—Heymann (portraits); Lekegian; both near Shepheard's Hotel.

Saddler.—F. J. Sauer.

English Tailors.—Collacott, Sharia-el-Manakh; Davies, Bryan and Co.; Lawson and Phillips, 19 Sharia-el-Maghraby.

Watchmaker and Jeweller.—Buys-Badollet, opposite Shepheard's Hotel; L. Kramer and Co., Rue Mooski.

Wine Merchants.—Walker and Co.; E. J. Fleurent, opposite Credit Lyonnais.

Shopping in Cairo is much simplified owing to most of the best shops being in the Rue Khamil Pasha, or two streets (Sharia-el-Maghraby and Sharia-el-Manakh) which lead out of the Place de l'Opéra, or in the Place de l'Opéra itself.

English Solicitor.—R. F. Wilme, Sharia-el-Maghraby.

Tourists' Agencies.—Messrs. Cook and Son, The Pavilion, Shepheard's Hotel; Henry Gaze and Sons, Limited, Rue Khamil Pasha.

III.—CAIRO AS A HEALTH RESORT

CAIRO itself cannot be unreservedly recommended as a health resort pure and simple. The Egyptian climate is undeniably admirably suited for a winter residence, and in most respects it is superior to that of any health resort in the South of France—the world's great winter sanatorium. But the city of Cairo possesses too many factitious drawbacks, which militate against its use as a climatic health station. Now that other health resorts, such as Luxor, Assouan, Helouan, etc., are getting better known and developed, medical men are beginning to realise that hygienically speaking Cairo is not Egypt. Its enormous population and limited area for one thing does not commend it to medical men as a winter residence for their patients. An over-crowded city of over 400,000 inhabitants, with its unsatisfactory hygienic conditions and appallingly primitive and unsanitary system of drainage—if system it can be called—the occasional visitation of cholera, etc., seems indeed the last place to which the health-seeker, as distinct from the mere tourist or pleasure-seeker, should be sent. It is true that the sanitation of the Continental, Shepheard's, Ghezireh Palace, and other fashionable hotels is beyond reproach, but then the visitor is not likely to spend the whole time in his hotel. Besides, the innumerable social gaieties and dissipations of this fashionable winter-city offer too many temptations to the invalid to neglect his health.

Twenty or thirty years ago, no doubt, the invalid had no choice: a winter in Egypt necessarily meant spending that season in Cairo. But now, thanks mainly to the enterprise of the great tourist agencies, Luxor, Assouan, and the Nile have been rendered available for delicate persons. The above remarks apply, of course, to the serious invalid as distinct from the large class of valetudinarians or "professional invalids." For this class of visitors, but more especially over-worked persons and those suffering from worry and "nerves," who require mainly change of scene and rest, Cairo with its innumerable resources and varied interests is an ideal wintering place. Besides, the above-mentioned objections to Cairo in the case of real invalids apply to those contemplating spending the whole winter in the city, and not merely a few weeks. The best disposal of time would be to spend the early winter months at Luxor or on a Nile voyage (for a whole winter on the Nile would be found monotonous) and postpone the return to Cairo till the beginning of February. November, December, and January are the least suitable months for Cairo, owing to the risk of malaria from the moisture arising from the subsiding inundation of the Nile. Then when Cairo gets too hot, Ramleh, near Alexandria, will be found an excellent intermediate health resort for a few weeks before leaving Egypt.

Helouan-les-Bains, within half an hour of Cairo by train, or Mena House at the foot of the Pyramids, would, however, be a better residence than Cairo itself. Helouan is, indeed, the oldest health resort in the world. There are about a dozen sulphur springs similar to those of Aix-les-Bains, but rather stronger. One of its chief merits is that those who have undergone a course at Aix can continue their "cure" here during the winter and spring, when, of course, the Aix establishment is closed. The atmosphere is remarkably pure and salubrious, and the electrical, tonic influence of the desert climate is felt here in a remarkable degree. There are good hotels here, two resident doctors, and several pensions. The Administration, too, have shown themselves thoroughly alive to the requirements of modern tourists, by providing lawn-tennis courts, laying down golf-links, etc. Hitherto the chief drawback was that the English guests were in a minority, the baths belonging to a German directorate. This is now changed. Another resort, which is strongly recommended by Dr. F. M. Sandwith, Dr. Hermann Weber, and other eminent climatologists, is Mena House at the Pyramids. Its advantages are thus summed up by Dr. Sandwith:—"Life at the large hotel here, numbering some 120 bedrooms, is for those who wish for purer air than that of crowded Cairo, but who desire to be within driving distance of their friends, and who dread the somewhat sombre monotony of Helouan. The Sphinx and the Pyramids, besides many attractions of their own, ensure a constant stream of visitors during the winter months. The air at both suburbs is probably equally pure and equally dry. For the comfort of the guests, there are provided a resident English doctor and chaplain, a chapel, a noble dining-room for 250 people, European chamber-maids, swimming bath, excellent conservancy arrangements, drinking water from a special well in the desert, steam laundry, a stringed band, books and magazines, billiard tables and photograph rooms. There are desert carts for driving, horses and camels for riding, occasional races, golf and lawn-tennis, and capital shooting from November to April. The climate of Helouan and the pyramids is much the same as in Cairo, except that the air is fresher, purer, and drier."

Then the Ghezireh Palace Hotel, with its famous gardens and shady avenues, far removed from the dust and glare of Cairo, though within frequent communication with the city, is in some respects a more suitable residence for delicate persons than the fashionable intra-mural hotels.

Whole volumes have been written by meteorologists and medical experts on the climatology of Egypt, but its chief characteristics can be summed up in a few words : a remarkably pure and salubrious atmosphere, almost continuous sunshine, rainlessness, —the rainfall of the Upper Nile valley is practically *nil*,—genial warmth (which, owing to its lack of moisture, is not oppressive), and highly tonic qualities; but, to counterbalance these good points, great lack of equability. The great difference between day and night temperatures is, no doubt, a very serious drawback. This lack of uniformity is, of course, inevitable in all countries where a high temperature and immunity from rain are combined. In short, it is a meteorological axiom that equability cannot exist with a very dry atmosphere and a high temperature. *Equability implies*, of course, *a certain amount of humidity.* An ideal climate would combine the equability and softness of Maderia, the warmth and dryness of Upper Egypt, and the chemically pure atmosphere of Biskra in Algeria.

The following summary of the climatic conditions of Cairo by Dr. F. M. Sandwith, prepared for my work on the health resorts of South Europe and North Africa (*Mediterranean Winter Resorts*, 3rd. ed. 1896), may be conveniently inserted here:—

"To save space, it is only necessary here to consider the seven winter months from 1st November to 31st May. The barometer seldom varies, though there is a steady fall from 29·99 in December to 29·82 in April. Rain amounts to one inch and a quarter, the number of days upon which drops or showers fall, being about fifteen. Clouds during January and February reach a maximum of 4 upon a scale from 0·10. The prevalent wind is from the north or north-west, and is never sufficiently fierce to keep patients within doors. The Khamseen blows from the south-west desert during March and April, seldom for more than two days in a week. It is unpleasantly hot and dusty while it lasts, and drives many visitors away from Cairo. The following table, drawn up from my own observations, shows the temperatures to which patients may be exposed. It is based on the principle that a sick man need not concern himself with the minimum *outdoor* temperature of a place, for that is always at an hour when he ought to be safe in bed. The vital information for him is the average maximum shade temperature out of doors, together with the average minimum bedroom heat, and the daily range between them. It will be noticed that there is no very serious range until the hot weather begins. My bedroom records have purposely been taken in a north room with door wide open, never visited by the sun, unoccupied at night, and unwarmed by artificial light. This, therefore, gives the greatest cold to which a patient can be subjected unless he opens his bedroom windows. A prudent invalid would, of course, eschew a north room, and would warm the air by lamp or candles on going to bed. Thus he would raise my minimum results some four degrees, and reduce the range of temperature considerably. It is interesting to note that my minimum results, within two or three degrees, correspond with the mean temperature of the month. During April and May it is, of course, easy to refrain from going out at the hottest time of the day. Thus it is evident that patients can spend six months in Cairo in a temperature which need only vary from 63° to 80°.

"The shortest days in December give us ten hours daylight, or three hours longer than in England.

	Temperature, Fahr. Maximum in Shade.	Minimum in Shade.	Rain.	Khamseen Wind.
November .	75 deg.	...	...	...
December .	69	60 deg.	4 days.	...
January . .	67·4	59·8	Showers 4 days.	...
February .	68·3	59·7	Showers 2 days.	2 days.
March . .	76	63·2	Drops 1 day.	3 ,,
April . .	84·5	67·6	Drops 2 days.	7·5 ,,
May . .	91·7	72	...	5·5 ,, "

The mere fact that for one absolutely cloudless winter day in the British Islands—even in the sunniest region of the south coast—there are ten or a dozen in Upper Egypt, means more, however, to the non-scientific reader than whole columns of meteorological readings and climatic statistics. In short, Egypt, and especially the Upper Nile, boasts of the most wonderful and salubrious climate of any known winter resort in the world, available to phthisical patients. There is, of course, no ideal climate on the surface of the globe—no hygienic Utopia where "the consumptive can draw in healing influences with every breath," but certainly the climate of Upper Egypt is the nearest approach, within ten days or so of London, to Tennyson's legendary land of Avalon,

> Where falls not rain, or hail, or any snow,
> Nor ever wind blows loudly.

Though the weather is popularly supposed to be the Englishman's staple topic of conversation, the ignorance of the veriest A B C of meteorology found among ordinarily well-informed and observant travellers is extraordinary. In Egyptian books of travel and magazine articles one occasionally finds the very quality in which the climate of Egypt is so deficient —equability of temperature—singled out along with its undeniable dryness for special praise.

Messrs. Hermann Weber, Burdon-Sanderson, C. Theodore Williams, F. M. Sandwith, and other physicians who have devoted considerable attention to the hygienic aspect of Egypt are agreed that Egypt is particularly suitable for most forms of lung disease, for incipient pulmonary consumption, chronic bronchitis, asthma, anæmia, chronic rheumatism, and, speaking generally, convalescents from acute diseases. But patients suffering from advanced heart disease, or, in short, very advanced disease of any organ, or from fever, should not be sent to Egypt. Persons subject to obstinate insomnia will also find the climate unsuitable.

With regard to the best way of reaching Egypt for invalids, though most travellers arrive by way of Port Said or Ismailia, this route is less preferable than *viâ* Alexandria for those who are wintering abroad for their health. The Egyptian tourist traffic is of slight importance compared to that of India and Australia in the eyes of the directors of the great liners, and passengers who have rashly decided to disembark for Cairo at Ismailia often find themselves landed at this half-way house in the middle of the night, with no means of reaching the capital till the next day. What is merely a passing inconvenience to the robust traveller might naturally be a serious matter for the invalid. The light railway which now runs from Port Said to Ismailia can, no doubt, be made use of, if the steamer arrives early in the day at Port Said, but the service is slow and infrequent. Though dignified by the name of railway, it is little more than a miniature steam tramway with a gauge of no more than two feet six inches. What is wanted is a railway from Port Said to Damietta, only forty miles west, whence there is direct railway communication to Cairo and Alexandria.

There are no physical difficulties in the construction of this much-needed railway. The real difficulty is the jealous opposition of Alexandria. Then, too, the Egyptian Government is not inclined to regard the scheme favourably, as the increased harbour dues would fall into the coffers of the Suez Canal Company and not into the Government Treasury. The fact remains that, as an ordinary commercial harbour, Port Said is of trifling importance. It is mainly an international port and coaling station.

Though Alexandria should be the port of arrival

for delicate persons, unfortunately the great passenger steamship Companies, such as the Peninsular and Oriental, Orient, and North German Lloyd make Port Said and not Alexandria their port of call in their through service. The increasing importance of the Egyptian passenger traffic has, however, induced the P. and O. Company to put on a special line of steamers, sailing every fortnight during the Egyptian tourist season, from London to Alexandria. Particulars of this service have already been given.

IV.—SOCIAL CAIRO[1]

CAIRO is emphatically a many-sided city, and may be described under many aspects. It is a famous historical city, an official capital, an important garrison town, and a great Oriental metropolis—in population the second city in the Turkish Empire. But by most visitors it is regarded merely as a fashionable winter health and pleasure resort. In fact as a *ville d'hiver*, if regarded in the two-fold aspect of a *ville de plaisir* and a *ville du beau monde*, it takes the highest rank among winter resorts, though, as we have shown, as an invalid station pure and simple, its repute is diminishing.

Its vogue as a winter residence for Europeans, may be said to date from the opening of the Suez Canal in 1869, when Cairo was boomed, to use a modern phrase, for all it was worth by the Khedive Ismail. This prodigal sovereign spent enormous sums in his attempts to convert his semi-Oriental capital into a kind of African Paris. Yet compare

[1] From an article contributed to *The Queen*.

Cairo of to-day as a fashionable tourist centre, with Cairo of a quarter of a century ago. Then the unfinished Esbekiyeh quarter had the appearance of a hastily run up suburb, and it was thought a remarkable achievement to light the streets with gas. Now the chief shops and all the large hotels are lit with electricity, and electric tram-cars run through the principal thoroughfares. It is even proposed to drain the picturesque, but decidedly malodorous and insalubrious Khalig Canal, which runs through the heart of the city from Old Cairo to Abbassieh, and convert it into an electric tramway. No doubt, artists and æsthetic tourists will rave at this Vandalistic measure, but the more thoughtful will not regret that what is virtually an open—and, in the summer, a pestiferous—sewer, should be transformed into an important highway of the greatest benefit to the teeming Cairene population, to say nothing of the inevitable improvement in public health which will result from the closing of the Canal. The Cairenes, it may be observed, in spite of their instinctive conservatism, take very kindly to these new forms of locomotion, so much so that, in the electric trams already running, foreign visitors are often crowded out by natives.

In some respects, so far as concerns the permanent

residents, society at Cairo resembles that of Simla and other fashionable haunts of Indian society, so large is the infusion of the military and official element. For society here has a decidedly official tone, and introductions are advisable if visitors wish to take part in the social life of the place, with its innumerable gaieties and entertainments of all kinds, from moonlight donkey-rides to the Pyramids to bicycle gymkhanas at the Ghezireh Palace, or fancy dress balls at Shepheard's or the Continental. In Cairo, however, the guests at the principal hotels form a society of their own. The hotel element in Cairo is a factor of greater importance in the social life of the foreign community, than at the fashionable winter resorts in the south of Europe, partly because the richer class of visitors, instead of living in isolated villas haughtily aloof from the cosmopolitan crowd of hotel-guests at Cairo, frequent the fashionable hotels. Villas, indeed, are here so scarce as to be practically unobtainable, the few there are being occupied by the families of the *Corps Diplomatique*, high Government officials, etc. In Egypt, indeed, dahabeahs may be said to take the place of villas.

In a sketch, then, of fashionable Cairo, some prominence must be given to the hotels. Shepheard's or the Continental might, indeed, be said to take the place of the Casino or Kursaal of continental watering-places. Each serves as a kind of social focus or rallying-place of the English community, and to a certain extent as a link between the winter residents and the tourists. Indeed, a lengthened stay at either of these fashionable hotels may almost be regarded, like membership of the *Cercle Nautique* at Cannes, or the Union Club at Malta, as a passport into Cairo society. Shepheard's is, in short, more of a cosmopolitan residential club than an ordinary hotel—a club, too, without its usual drawbacks of an entrance fee and risk of black-balling.

This unique feature is especially indicated by the numerous notices of entertainments and social functions which are posted up in the entrance hall. Side by side with the advertisement of a polo pony or hack for sale, or of a dahabeah to let, may be seen a list of the meetings of the Turf Club, a notice of a forthcoming gymkhana, a charity bazaar at the English Agency, or a fancy dress ball at the Continental. Then English officers quartered at Cairo, seem by prescriptive right to have the run of Shepheard's, and even the General Orders are posted here as conspicuously and as regularly as at Kasr-en-Nil or Abbassieh Barracks. It might be supposed from this, that there were no good clubs at Cairo

The fashionable season is a short one, lasting from January to April. The flight of the European visitors to cooler climes during this month is soon followed by the exodus of the official world and other permanent residents to Ramleh and other summer refuges. The Khedive and his household usually leave for Alexandria about the beginning of May, and this departure of the titular sovereign formally marks the close of the Cairo season. The ordinary season for tourists begins earlier, and its duration is sufficiently indicated by the period during which the principal hotels are open, which is from the beginning of November to the end of April.

V.—HOTELS AND HOTEL LIFE

THE leading hotels in Cairo, headed by the historical Shepheard's and the luxurious Continental, can certainly compare favourably with the best hotels of the most fashionable Riviera watering-places. Leaving the United States out of the question, it is perhaps hardly going too far to say that no extra-European city of the same size offers such a wide choice of high-class and well-appointed hotels so well adapted to meet the demands of English travellers as the "City of the Caliphs." The invidious task of classifying them is fairly easy, for they naturally fall into three categories.

In the first rank are Shepheard's, Continental, New, Mena House (Pyramids), and the new Ghezireh Palace Hotel. These are all fashionable houses, with commensurate prices. There is one uniform charge of sixteen *shillings* (not *francs*) a day, for the American system of *pension* charges is almost universal in Cairo. But it must be allowed, as some excuse for these undeniably high charges—judged, that is, from a European standpoint—that these prices obtain only during the more fashionable months, January, February, and March. For the rest of the season the daily charge is generally reduced to fourteen shillings.

The most fashionable are undoubtedly the Continental, Shepheard's, and Ghezireh Palace, whose visitors' lists almost suggest a page out of the *Almanac de Gotha.* Yet as regards the *clientèle* each has a distinct character of its own, and if I may attempt a somewhat invidious task I should be inclined to state that the Continental is more peculiarly exclusive and aristocratic, while Shepheard's is smarter and the note of modernity here is more insistent. As for the Ghezireh Palace Hotel it is of too recent date to have acquired any distinct social characteristics. The salient features of these establishments may perhaps be better understood by comparison with London hotels. The Continental, then, may be compared with the Alexandra or the Albemarle, Shepheard's with the Savoy, and the Ghezireh Palace with the Cecil.

The historical Shepheard's has a world-wide reputation. It must, however, be remembered that not a stone remains of the old Shepheard's, with its world-renowned balcony, its garden containing the tree under which General Kleber was assassinated, its lofty rooms and terraces. The new Shepheard's, completely rebuilt in 1891, lacks these historical adjuncts, but the high reputation for comfort remains, and certainly in point of luxury and refinements of civilisation, in the form of electric lights, lifts, telephones, etc., there can be no comparison. No doubt there was a touch of Oriental romance, and a suggestion of the "Thousand and One Nights," in the time-honoured practice which formerly obtained at Shepheard's of summoning the dusky attendants by clapping the hands; but to the matter-of-fact latter-day traveller the prosaic, but reliable, electric bell is an infinitely preferable means of communication.

Shepheard's is *par excellence* the American hotel, while the Continental is more exclusively English. The latter, too, partakes more of the character of a high-class residential family hotel, its numerous elegantly appointed suites of private apartments (some twenty sets) being one of its leading features.

Shepheard's *clientèle* is distinctly cosmopolitan. Cairo being the starting-point for the Desert, the Nile, and Palestine, and not far off the high road to India and Australia, and also being one of those cities which no self-respecting globe-trotter can afford to omit in his round, it is much visited by passing travellers. Shepheard's, on account of its associations and traditions, is a favourite resort of Anglo-Indians and officers of both services. Those, however, purposing to spend the whole season in Cairo would be more likely to go to the Continental or the Ghezireh Palace. To visitors of a retiring disposition what are usually thought the great charms of Shepheard's, its central situation, its life and gaiety—for afternoon tea on the terrace is quite an institution of Cairo society—are regarded rather as drawbacks. It is undoubtedly very central and easy of access, but, fronting the main road, it is unpleasantly noisy and dusty. In the old days there were no doubt compensations in the moving panorama of Oriental life which this crowded thoroughfare presented, a kaleidosocopic procession of Bedouin Arabs from the desert, camels, tattooed negroes, Turks, jewelled pashas ambling past on richly-caparisoned mules, mysterious veiled figures, and other fascinating aspects of Eastern life, with a very slight admixture of the vulgarising (artistically speaking) European element. Now, instead of these picturesque motley crowds, the modern lounger on the famous terraces looks down upon a yelling crowd of donkey-boys, guides, porters, interpreters, dragomans, itinerant dealers in sham antiques, and all the noisy rabble that live on the travelling Briton.

The Continental Hotel is comparatively new, while the New Hotel is one of the oldest hotels in Cairo; but this instance of erratic hotel nomenclature is not confined to Egypt. It is most sumptuously decorated, and the appointments are quite as luxurious as those of the leading hotels at the fashionable watering-places on the opposite shore of the Mediterranean. Special mention should be made of the excellence of its sanitary arrangements. It is situated in a quiet part of the fashionable Esbekiyeh quarter, near the English Church, and is no doubt a little out-of-the-way compared with Shepheard's and the New hotels; but it must be confessed that this comparative remoteness is regarded as an additional recommendation by many of its patrons.

The Ghezireh Palace, formerly known as "Ismail's Folly," the newest of the Cairo hotels, was one of the palaces of the late Khedive Ismail, whose mania for building palaces was as pronounced as that of the unfortunate King of Bavaria. It was bought by a syndicate from the creditors of the late ex-Khedive, and is now one of the International Palace Hotels—a commercial enterprise which is a worthy rival of the Gordon Hotels ring—belonging to the International Sleeping Car Company. The Palace, though modern, is of great historic interest. It was enlarged and decorated at enormous expense by the Khedive Ismail for the entertainment of his royal guests who were lodged here at the opening of the Suez Canal, including the Empress Elizabeth, the Empress Eugénie, and the Prince of Wales. It rivals the Continental or Shepheard's in the costliness of its decoration and the luxury of its appointments. From a medical point of view its strong points are its delightfully rural, and at the same time readily accessible, situation, and its sheltered position, which effectually protects visitors from the occasional Khamseen winds—rare, no doubt, but still to be reckoned with during the Cairo season. As regards its visitors the Ghezireh Palace is perhaps rather more cosmopolitan in character than the Continental or even Shepheard's. The charming gardens and park deserve special mention. Probably no hotel in Europe can compare with Ghezireh Palace in this respect. A striking feature of the pleasure-grounds is the kiosque, used as a casino, with ball-room, billiard-room, and restaurant. This is evidently modelled on the Alcazar of Seville, and according to Baedeker is the finest modern Arabian structure of its kind. In front are a lake, fountains, aviaries, etc., while between the kiosque and the Shubra Avenue—the fashionable drive of Cairo—is an ornamental park laid out with considerable taste. Then there is a terrace fronting the Nile which makes a particularly pleasant lounge with its views of the ever-varying river traffic.

Certainly there is room for an extra-mural hotel at Cairo, with its swarms of invalids increasing year by year who invade Egypt for the winter, and it should appeal not only to this numerically important class, but also to sportsmen, owing to its vicinity to the race-course and the Sporting Club grounds.

In 1897 this hotel was amalgamated with Shepheard's, and they are now the property of a Company called "The Egyptian Hotels, Limited," who have leased them to the International Sleeping Car Company.

So much, then, for the three leading Cairo hotels. We now come to another first-class hotel. The New Hotel was the favourite *caravanserai* of the ex-Khedive Ismail, and it occupies by far the best situation of any in Cairo, facing the Grand Opera House. It has had vicissitudes, but has recovered and stood the test of time, and not being so popular as Shepheard's and the Continental, which are often overcrowded in the height of the season, it might be preferred by invalids and those in need of rest and quietness. Its numerous sets of upper rooms, each furnished with an alcoved balcony, might also recommend it to this class of visitors.

Mena House, at the foot of the Pyramids, is a large and expensive establishment, which has found favour with our compatriots. No doubt those with the artistic sense highly developed will enlarge on the enormity of building a huge modern hotel in the midst of such incongruous surroundings, in the close vicinity of the immortal Pyramids and the mystic Sphinx; but it must be admitted, if I may be permitted to act as *advocatus diaboli*, that if the Pyramids had to be vulgarised they could not have been vulgarised better (or less) by the English capitalist who is responsible for the undertaking.

The origin of Mena House (called from Menes, the quasi-mythical earliest king of Egypt) is curious. Some seven years ago an Englishman in delicate health came to Egypt. He built a tiny house under the shadow of the Pyramids. Finding the air beneficial, he began to erect a small sanatorium, hoping that invalids like himself might resort there, and gain a longer lease of life. But before the plan was matured he died. Then Mr. Locke-King bought the property, and determined to start a hotel. The undertaking grew under his hands, and now Mena House may be considered to rank as one of the leading hotels in Egypt. Mr. Locke-King, however, no longer owns the Mena House, having transferred his interest therein to an English syndicate. It is well spoken of and the rooms are furnished in good taste. It is well appointed and is furnished with a large swimming bath, English billiard table, library, etc. Golf links are also duly advertised among its numerous attractions for visitors, though considering the general lay of the desert surrounding the Pyramids "sporting bunkers" must be too plentiful even for the most determined devotee of the "royal and ancient game," and the laying out of anything approaching to a putting-green must have presented almost insuperable difficulties. There is a resident chaplain and physician.

This hotel is popular with visitors of sporting tastes, as very tolerable quail shooting can be had in the spring (see chapter on "Sport") within a few minutes of the hotel.

The second category includes the medium-priced hotel with a charge of twelve shillings a day—viz. Angleterre, Royal, and Du Nil.

The Hotel d'Angleterre is a favourite resort of English and Americans, while the two latter have a large proportion of French and Germans among their guests. It is a particularly comfortable and well-managed house, and is under the same proprietorship as the Continental. It has recently been rebuilt, and is furnished with all modern conveniences—lift, electric light, etc.—in fact, it is a second

Continental on a more modest scale, and may almost be regarded as a *succursale* or *dependance* of the parent establishment.

The Hotel Royal may be said to have some claims on the gratitude of Englishmen. During Arabi's rebellion, all the hotel-keepers, save the landlord of the "Royal," decamped. Thus, after the victorious campaign, the English officers would have fared badly had not the doors of the "Royal" been open to them. This hotel has a good reputation for its *cuisine* and moderate charges. There remains the well-known old-established Hotel du Nil, handicapped a little, however, by its situation close to the malodorous street known as the Mooski. This hotel, well known to scholars, literary men, and Egyptologists, boasts of a famous garden, one of the most beautiful and striking in Cairo. In the opinion of many of its guests, this lovely pleasure-ground, which shuts off all noises from the crowded streets, quite compensates for its proximity to the native quarter.

The third group of hotels, with prices from twelve shillings downwards, consists of the Bristol, Villa Victoria, Métropole, Khedivial, Voyageurs, and Ismailia. Of these the first three are most frequented by English travellers. These are more of the class of hotel pensions than those I have described above.

The Bristol and Métropole are the latest additions to the Cairo hotels. They are quite up to the requirements of modern tourists, have electric light, etc. The Bristol was built in 1894, and is provided with a lift. It faces the Esbekiyeh Gardens, while the Métropole is near the Place de l'Opéra. The pension charge at each is 10s., while the Villa Victoria charges 12s. a day.

There are several boarding-houses or private *pensions*, such as Villa Fink, Villa Konig, and Villa Couteret. The prices are certainly very moderate for Cairo (eight to ten shillings a day), but they cannot be unreservedly recommended to English visitors, as they are under German proprietorship, and frequented chiefly by visitors of that nationality.

The hotels Shepheard, Royal, Du Nil, and many of the cheaper houses, are kept open all through the year. The above, with the Continental, Ghezireh Palace, Mena House, and Khedivial, accept Cook's hotel coupons, while those of Messrs. Gaze are taken by the Hotels d'Angleterre and Métropole. Speaking generally, the average of accommodation, service, attendance, and *cuisine* at the best hotels is high. The service, in especial, is better and more plentiful than at hotels of similar standing in Europe, owing mainly to labour being cheap. The best hotels are decidedly expensive, but then it must be remembered that they cater for a richer class of visitors, taken as a whole, than would be found at most of the winter resorts of the South of Europe. Those who wish to spend the winter in the South with the strictest economy rarely visit Egypt. Not only is the daily *pension* charge high, but the incidental items in the hotel bills are very expensive. For instance, the charge for washing a dozen collars or handkerchiefs would be 2s. 6d. Tips, too, rule higher than in European hotels. But the most objectionable feature in Egyptian hotel life is the universal *baksheesh* system, which seems to find particularly congenial soil in the Cairo hotels. It is certainly advisable, however, for hotel visitors to conform to this custom of the country if they care for their personal comfort.

Apartments can be obtained by the month in the Esbekiyeh quarter and elsewhere. The rents are very high. The charges for a bed and sitting-room vary from 120 fr. to 175 fr. a month.

Villas.—Furnished villas can be rented for the season, but the terms are high and the supply limited. The usual rent for a furnished villa with ten rooms in the Ismailia quarter is £30 or £40 per month. These villas are mostly of European architecture, not Moorish as in Algiers.

VI.—THE MOSQUES

THOUGH, next to the bazaars, the mosques are in the opinion of the Cairo guides the chief lions of Cairo, yet it must be allowed that the ordinary visitor will find a whole day devoted solely to these Moslem temples somewhat tedious. It is certainly advisable to combine the excursion to the mosques with some other kind of sight-seeing. Those who are pressed for time could easily combine an inspection of many of the mosques with a visit to the bazaars, for half a dozen of the most interesting are within a short distance of the junction of the Rue Neuve (the continuation of the Mooski), and Suk-en-Nahassin, the centre of the bazaar quarter, viz. Ghuri, Hassanen, En Nasr Mohammed (not to be confounded with the mosque of the same name in the Citadel), Kalaun, Barkukiyeh, and El-Azhar.

The Mameluke sovereigns were great mosque builders, and it will be noticed that the most interesting mosques date from the end of the thirteenth century to the beginning of the sixteenth (when the Ottoman Sultan, Selim II., conquered Egypt), which synchronizes with the Golden Age of the two Mameluke dynasties.

The principal features of a mosque are an open court (*sahn*) with a fountain in the middle, used by the Moslems for ablutions—a necessary preliminary to Moslem worship—surrounded by a covered cloister (*liwan*). The more sacred part of the building, (*maksura*), which corresponds to the choir of a Christian cathedral, is usually screened off from the rest of the building, and here the tomb of the founder is usually placed. In the centre of this sanctuary is the niche (*mihrab*) showing the direction of Mecca, and the pulpit (*mimbar*). It is necessary to remember these principal portions of a Mohammedan temple if an intelligent grasp of Moslem ecclesiastical architecture is to be obtained. But it must be remembered that many of the Cairo mosques do not approximate to this normal type, and unfortunately the most correct, architecturally speaking, mosques in Cairo, viz. Amru, Ibn Tulun, and El-Azhar, are either in ruins or have been restored out of all resemblance to the original structure. "Speaking generally," says Dr. Wallis Budge, "there are three types of mosque in Cairo. (1) Courtyard surrounded by colonnades (Amru and Tulun); (2) Courtyard surrounded by four arches (Sultan Hassan); (3) Court covered with dome (Mohammed Ali)."

There are over three hundred mosques in Cairo—indeed, it is said by the Arabs that, as in the case of the churches of Rome, there is one for every day of the year—but most are in ruins; a large number have been laicised, and there remain scarcely over a score that even the most conscientious sight-seer would care to explore. The best worth visiting are Amru (Old Cairo), Mohammed Ali (Citadel), Tulun, Kalaun, Sultan Hassan, El-Hakim (Arab Museum), El-Akbar (Tekiyet), El-Hassanen, Ibrahim Agha, El-Ghuri, Abu Bekr, El-Azhar (Moslem University), El Muaiyad, and the tomb-mosques of Kait Bey, El-Ashraf Bursbey, and Barkuk (Tombs of the Caliphs). In some of the larger mosques, such as Kalaun, a whole group of public buildings are comprised: besides the mosque proper, there will be found a hospital, school, court of justice, monastery, library, etc.

A ticket (price two piastres), which can be usually obtained from the hotel porter, is required for visiting all the mosques, but El-Azhar is not always accessible even with a ticket. For some of the mosques it is necessary to obtain the ticket at the Wakfs Office (Administration of the Mosques) in the Place Abdin.

The proceeds of the tickets are devoted to the fund for the restoration of the mosques. Then at each mosque a gratuity of two piastres will have to be given for the loan of slippers. Four or five piastres are often demanded of English visitors but two are quite sufficient. It will be seen then that a systematic tour of the mosques is rather a costly undertaking.

Itinerary of the Mosques.—Those who wish to do all the principal mosques within the walls (for the Citadel and Tombs of the Caliphs require a separate visit) in one excursion should take a donkey for the whole morning (ten or twelve piastres) and follow this itinerary, simply telling the donkey-boy the name of the desired mosque in turn, and directing him to show the nearest way to each.

By this means a hurried tourist can visit the principal mosques in about four hours. It would be better, of course, to devote two mornings to this tour, taking the mosques south of the Mooski one morning, and the mosques north of this thoroughfare the next morning.

Starting from the Place de l'Opéra and making for the Place du Mooski, as the junction of the Rue Neuve and Suk-en-Nahassin is now officially termed, take the mosques in the following order:—El-Ghuri, El-Azhar, Muaiyad, El-Akbar, Tulun, Sultan

Hassan, Ibrahim Agha, Hassanen, Muristan Kalaun, Mohammed-en-Nasr, Barkukiyeh, Abu-Bekr, and El-Hakim.

If two mornings can be given to the mosques, on the first morning the tour might end with Ibrahim Agha, and on the second morning a start could be made with Hassanen Mosque, and after El-Hakim there would be time for a visit to the Tombs of the Caliphs and Burckhardt's Tomb.

El-Ghuri.—This charming little mosque, though close to the Attarin Bazaar and easy of access, is not so much visited by Europeans as it should be. It was built by the Sultan El-Ghuri, one of the most enlightened of the Circassian Mameluke Sultans, who reigned 1501 to 1516 A.D. The coloured marbles on the walls and floor are particularly fine. The restorations carried out here by the Commission for the Preservation of Arabic Monuments reflect considerable credit on this body.

El-Azhar.—This huge building is unique among the Cairene mosques. It is the largest Moslem university in the world, and one of the oldest, for the old mosque was set apart for study towards the end of the tenth century. Over eleven thousand scholars and three hundred professors are said to be "inscribed on the books" of this ancient foundation. On Friday, the Mohammedan Sabbath, no teaching takes place, and as this is its most salient feature, strangers should choose some other day for their visit. The authorities do not altogether encourage the presence of strangers, and even when armed with the official permit from the Wakfs, there is sometimes a difficulty in gaining admittance.

Some of the sects—and all the chief Moslem sects are represented in this truly Catholic Institution—are decidedly fanatical, and strangers will be well advised to abstain from any overt expression of amusement at the extraordinary spectacle of some thousands of students of all ages, repeating verses of the Koran in a curious monotone, while swaying their bodies from side to side—supposed to be an aid to memory.

The vast proportions of the building, the dim light, low roof, and the numerous pillars (nearly 400) remind the tourist of Cordova Cathedral, perhaps the best preserved and most perfect specimen of this form of Saracenic art in existence.

Muaiyad.—This is popularly known as the Red Mosque. It is close to the Bab-es-Zuwellah, which artists will no doubt consider one of the most picturesque bits of Cairo. The magnificent bronze gate at the entrance was formerly in the Sultan Hassan Mosque. This mosque was built by El-Muaiyad (1412-21 A.D.). It has been recently restored.

El-Akbar.—Architecturally this mosque is of slight interest, but is much visited, as here the Friday performances of the Dancing Dervishes take place (see chapter on "Minor Sights").

Ibn Tulun.—This mosque is, next to the Amru mosque—the mother-mosque of Cairo—the oldest in Cairo, and being in a very ruinous state it is more attractive to the archæologist or the historian, than to the ordinary tourist. Like the Agia Sophia (St. Sophia) of Constantinople, it was designed by a Christian architect, and is said to be a copy of the Kaaba of Mecca. It was built by Sultan Tulun, the founder of the Tulunide Dynasty (868 to 895 A.D.), but little of the original building remains. A great wealth of legendary lore clusters round this venerable building, and, according to the chroniclers, it is built on the site of the Burning Bush, Abraham's sacrifice, and the landing-place of the Ark!

A curious feature of the building is the pointed arches which recall the Norman style of architecture. The minaret is a striking feature of the exterior. It has an amusing legend attached to it. According to the Arabic tradition its shape—a ram's horn—is thus explained. Ibn El-Tulun was one day holding a council, and played thoughtlessly as he sat at table with a sheet of paper which he unconsciously kept folding and unfolding. When he recovered from this fit of abstraction, he noticed his officers and councillors looking at him, curiously surprised at his absence of mind. In order to efface the bad impression, he pretended that what looked like childishness was really profound thought, and again carefully twisting the paper he gave it to the architect of the mosque, and told him that he wished the minaret to take that form.

Sultan Hassan.—This is the great show-mosque of Cairo, and its most striking features are its vast proportions. It is a colossal building, and is said to have cost over £600,000. In a certain sense it may be considered the national mosque of Cairo. It has often served as a kind of meeting-place of the populace in times of public disturbance, and a rallying-place of demagogues and opponents of the Government, notably in the case of the so-called National Movement in 1881.

The body of the Sultan who was assassinated in 1361, lies in a mausoleum beneath a dome nearly two hundred feet high.

The following description of this majestic building, from an article in the *Art Journal*, will give an idea of its enormous proportions :—

The outer walls of this stately mosque are nearly 100 feet in height, and they are capped by a cornice 13 feet high, projecting 6 feet, formed of stalactite, which has ever since been a marked feature in Arabian architecture.

The arches of the doorways and of the numerous windows, and even the capitals of the columns, are similarly enriched. The great doorway in the northern side is situated in a recess 66 feet in height. The minaret, gracefully converted from a square at its base to an octagon in its upper part, is the loftiest in existence, measuring 280 feet.

This noble building is unfortunately in a very ruinous condition, but instead of restoring it the late Khedive confined his energies to building the adjoining mosque of the Rifaiya, which was intended to rival the Mosque of Sultan Hassan.

Ibrahim Agha.—One of the most attractive mosques is that popularly known as Ibrahim Agha, or by tourists, "the Blue-tiled Mosque," from the colour of the tiles with which it is profusely decorated. Its official title is Kherbek, as it was built by this renegade Mameluke, who afterwards became the first Pasha of Egypt under the Ottoman Sultans. On this account it is not surprising that the Cairenes have not wished to perpetuate the name of the founder, and prefer to call the mosque after Ibrahim Agha, who enlarged and restored it in 1617. The interior is well described by Colonel Plunkett in his slight but charming little *brochure*, "Walks in Cairo":—"The vaulted colonnade on the east side rests on massive piers, and between them glows the rich blue of the tiles which cover the wall; they are set in panels, though somewhat irregularly, and with some serious gaps where doubtless unscrupulous collectors have obtained valuable specimens by the aid of dishonest guardians. The effect depends greatly on the light by which the mosque is seen, but is always rich and striking; the open court, too, with its little garden of palms and other trees in the centre, and the graceful minaret rising above the crenellated wall, is very attractive, and has, especially towards sunset, a peculiarly quiet and beautiful appearance."

El-Hassanen.—This mosque is dedicated to Hassan and Hassein, the two sons of Ali (son-in-law of Mahomet). These grandsons of the Prophet have been virtually canonised by Moslems, and this mosque is held to possess peculiar sanctity. The mosque has been completely rebuilt, and is now lighted with gas, but the old dome which covers the mausoleum of Hassein has been preserved. The guide will point out the column which is said to contain the head of the saint.

Kalaun.—This is one of the largest mosques in Cairo. It is not, however, strictly a mosque but a hospital (Muristan). It was built by the Sultan Kalaun (1279-90 A.D.). It is in a very ruinous condition. The only object of interest is the mausoleum of the founder. Certain relics of the Sultan are preserved here, though they cannot, of course, be seen by Christians. These relics are held to possess, of course, miraculous properties by the devout, and this mosque is a renowned place of pilgrim resort. The mausoleum chamber is architecturally of considerable interest, and is better preserved than most of these mausolea. It is a square with a central octagon and dome. The kibla (prayer-recess) is elaborately decorated with coloured marbles and mother-of-pearl.

En Nasr Mohammed.—The adjoining mosque was built by Mohammed, the son of Sultan Kalaun, in 1303. The pointed doorway is particularly noticeable and shows a trace of the Gothic influence introduced by the Crusaders. This beautiful gateway was brought as a trophy from a Christian church at Acre built by the Crusaders, and would not, as Mr. Stanley Lane-Poole aptly observes, "be out of place in Salisbury Cathedral."

Barkukiyeh.—The adjoining mosque, the last of the famous triad of mosques, whose façades form such a striking and picturesque architectural group, is also a tomb-mosque. Here are buried the wife and daughter of the Sultan Barkuk (1382-99 A.D.), the first of the Circassian slave dynasty. The exquisite bronze workmanship of one of the doors should be specially noticed. The tomb of the Sultan himself is in the tomb-mosque in the eastern cemetery (see "Tombs of the Caliphs").

Abu Bekr.—This is one of the most beautifully decorated mosques in Cairo. It is rather neglected by the generality of tourists, partly perhaps because the guide-books dismiss it with very scant notice. But a visit will be well repaid. The marble mosaics are perhaps unequalled in Cairo. The mosque has recently been admirably restored by Herz Bey, the architect of the Wakfs Commission, who has carried out the work with scrupulous fidelity to the original design. The result is an architectural gem.

El-Hakim.—This is one of the largest as well as the oldest mosques, but it is in a deplorably ruinous condition. It is visited chiefly as the temporary refuge of the Museum of Arabic Art (see "Museum" chapter). For many years the objects in this unique collection were stowed away in one of the mosque buildings without any attempt at systematic or chronological arrangement, and were lost to most visitors, but recently the authorities have had the objects carefully arranged and scientifically catalogued. The mosque is unique as being the sole one provided with a Makhara (an external platform not to be confounded with a minaret), on which incense is burned on important festivals. El-Hakim, the founder, belonged to the Tulunide dynasty, and founded the sect of the Druses. He reigned 996-1021 A.D. The mosque was completed in 1003 A.D.

This concludes the sketch of the most noteworthy mosques within the walls of Cairo. The mosques of the Citadel, old Cairo, and of the Tombs of the Caliphs will be described separately.

VII.—THE BAZAARS

A VISIT to the bazaar region is one of the most interesting and instructive excursions within the walls. But its great charm is lost if a set itinerary is laid down, and if it is merely regarded as one of the principal items in the round of sight-seeing. The right way to appreciate the bazaars is to make no fixed plan, and certainly to dispense with a dragoman or interpreter. It is also preferable to visit them on foot and not on donkey-back.

But though a fixed itinerary is to be deprecated, yet it is well to get some idea beforehand of their topography, for if once the visitor asks the way he will find it difficult to shake off the crowd of donkey-boys and loafing guides who will insist on offering their services. The boundaries and main arteries of the bazaar can easily be mastered in spite of the apparently inextricable maze of narrow lanes and alleys, for they are intersected by two main thoroughfares and have well-defined boundaries. One of these main highways is generally known by the name of Suk-en-Nahassin, from its principal bazaar, and is called by different names according to the bazaars which bound it. It is one of the narrowest and oldest but most important of the streets of Cairo, and extends from the Mosque el-Hakim, close to the Bab-en-Nasr, to the Boulevard Mehemet Ali, the broad, modern street which runs direct from the Esbekiyeh Square to the Citadel. The other main street is the Rue Neuve, the prolongation of the Mooski which leads to the Tombs of the Caliphs. The Mooski was the Frankish or foreign quarter before Ismail built the modern European district which radiates from the Esbekiyeh Square.

Some of the bazaars cluster round large covered market-places called khans, of which the most important are the Khan Khalil, between the Hassanen Mosque and the junction of the Suk-en-Nahassin and the Rue Neuve, and the Khan Gamaliyeh near the Bab-en-Nasr.

Tourists who have only a short time to devote to Cairo, and others to whom the advice to visit the bazaars without any fixed plan or itinerary would be considered a counsel of perfection, would find that the most expeditious method of exploring the bazaars would be to start from the Khan Khalil, explore this highly picturesque quarter, and then visit the Khan Gamaliyeh. Then make for the Suk-en-Nahassin, and, using this street as a kind of movable base and proceeding down it towards the Rue Neuve, visit the more interesting bazaars which abound in this street, and continue till the Bab-es-Zuwellah is reached.

It must be remembered that the bazaars are less oriental in aspect than those of Damascus for instance, and Baedeker considers them inferior even to those of Constantinople. As in all oriental cities, each bazaar is confined as a rule to shops or booths for the sale of one class of goods only, or products of a certain district, from which the bazaar is usually named.

The Khan Khalil was built in 1292, by the famous Sultan El-Ashraf, the conqueror of Acre, on the site of the real Tombs of the Caliphs. It is the chief market for carpets, rugs, and embroidered stuffs. Open-air auctions, which are very amusing to watch, take place on the mornings of Monday and Thursday.

Crossing the street Suk-en-Nahassin, we come to the Suk-es-Saigh (gold and silversmiths' bazaar). The quality of the trinkets has much deteriorated of late; and many of the foreign residents declare that much that is sold here comes from the Palais Royal in Paris, or from Birmingham.

Going northwards, and turning to the right, we

reach the Gamaliyeh (camel-drivers) quarter, where the Red Sea traders are found. The goods they sell are very inferior, generally consisting of perfumes, spices, mother-of-pearl, and attar of roses; but the latter is so weak that they can sell for a franc a flask what would cost a pound if pure. The north of this street forms the coppersmiths' bazaar, and here are also booths for the sale of pipes and other articles for smokers.

Retracing our steps to the starting-point, and crossing the Rue Neuve (really one of the oldest streets) we reach the once flourishing Suk-es-Sudun. At present the name is a misnomer, for the Soudan has been practically closed to traders for many years. In this quarter are the booksellers' bazaar, of little interest, and the Suk-el-Attarin (spices, perfumes, etc.)

Unfortunately, in the bazaars mostly visited by strangers, the articles sold are either inferior imported goods from Europe, or cheap and showy bric-à-brac and sham curios. Thus many of the shops are like the oriental stalls at Exhibitions. Genuine oriental goods can, however, be bought at the picturesque Suk-el-Fahhamin, behind El-Ghuri Mosque, a favourite haunt of artists. Here are to be found rugs, bernouses, fez caps, etc., from Tunis, Algeria, and Morocco.

Hints to Purchasers.—In buying it is of course

necessary to try and make bargains. Even an inexperienced tourist had better trust to his own powers of bargaining rather than leave the matter in the hands of his guide. The seller has generally a different price for each customer. Some advise the purchaser always to offer *half* of what is asked; but dealers are fully aware of this device, and raise their original prices accordingly. A visitor, however, who has time and patience to spare, can often get real bargains: at any rate he can sometimes, by dint of protracted negotiations, secure valuable articles at reasonable prices. When buying jewellery, see that it has the Government stamp, indicating number of carats. Real mushrabiyeh work (carved wooden lattice-work) is very costly, and most specimens sold are sham. In the real thing (the most characteristic Cairo industry) each piece is irregular and cut by hand; but in the imitations they are turned by a lathe in one uniform size. The best times for seeing the bazaars are the early mornings and late afternoons of Mondays and Thursdays.

Even now, as far as bargaining is concerned, the time-honoured oriental methods prevail. The negotiations are hedged round with an amount of ceremony that recalls the stately fashion in the *Arabian Nights*, when the purchase of a brass tray or an embroidered saddle-cloth was a solemn treaty, and the bargain for a lamp a diplomatic event not to be lightly undertaken or hurriedly concluded by either of the high contracting parties. Those who are anxious to imbibe the oriental "atmosphere" will, no doubt, be more inclined to tolerate the tedious process of chaffering than the ordinary matter-of-fact tourist. Native manners and customs can be well observed in the region of the bazaars; for, as in all Eastern countries, the inhabitants live in the open air as much as possible. The El-Muaiyad Bazaar, being peculiarly a native mart, and one less frequented by tourists, is a particularly good field for the searcher after local colour.

But for broad effects, the visitor must betake himself to the Mooski, the most characteristic thoroughfare of Cairo; for here, indeed, the "East shakes hands with the West." This living diorama, formed by the brilliant and ever-shifting crowd, is quite unique. Not even in Constantinople, the most cosmopolitan city, in a spectacular sense, in Europe, can we find greater variety of nationalities. One seems to meet here every costume of Europe, Asia, and Africa; and the kaleidoscopic varieties of brilliant and fantastic colouring, are bewildering to a stranger. Solemn and impassive-looking Turks, gently ambling past on gaily-caparisoned mules, grinning negroes from the Soudan, melancholy-looking Fellahs in their scanty blue kaftans, cunning-featured Levantines, green-turbaned Shereefs, and picturesque Bedouins from the desert, stalking past in their flowing bernouses, make up the mass of this restless throng. A Sakkah, or water-carrier, carrying his picturesque goatskin filled with Nile water, still finds a sale for his ware, in spite of the public fountains; while among other *dramatis personæ* of the "Arabian Nights" are the vendors of sweets and other edibles. Gorgeously arrayed Jewesses, fierce-looking Albanians bristling with weapons, and petticoated Greeks, give variety of colour to this living kinetoscope. A white group of Egyptian ladies, totally concealed under the inevitable yashmak and voluminous haik, give a restful relief to this blaze of colour. Such are the elements in this mammoth masquerade which make up the brilliant picture of Cairene street life.

VIII.—THE NATIONAL MUSEUM

The National Museum of Antiquities is at Ghizeh, about three miles from the Esbekiyeh Square. It is usually reached by the new electric tramway which runs from the Central Station over the Kasr-en-Nil Bridge to the Museum. This tramway is to be continued to the Pyramids. It must be remembered, however, that the Nile Bridge (a drawbridge) is closed to allow of the river traffic passing from 1 P.M. to 2.45 P.M. Another route is by the electric tramway to Kasr-el-Aini Hospital (opposite Roda Island) and thence by ferry.

The Museum is open daily (except Friday) from 9.30 A.M. to 4.30 P.M. Admission 5 p., Tuesday free. Official Catalogue (French) 10 p. The ordinary visitor, however, who does not care to devote more than one morning to this vast treasure-house of art, will be well advised to dispense with a catalogue and resist the inclination to "do" the Museum thoroughly, and confine his energies to visiting only a few of the ninety rooms which compose the collection. Even to examine at all adequately one-tenth of the rooms, means a whole day's hard work.

The Palace of Ghizeh, which was once the Haremlik (Palace of the Harem) of the Khedive Ismail, has, since 1889, when the collection was removed from Boulaq, been the resting-place of the National Museum. But this huge palace, in spite of its many rooms, is not large enough for the proper display of the antiquities, and the building not being fire-proof, the Government are fully alive to the necessity of housing this invaluable collection in a fire-proof building constructed specially for a museum. The foundations of the building, close to the Kasr-en-Nil Bridge, were laid last April (1897), and it is expected that it will be completed by March 1899.

The Museum contains not only the largest but the most valuable collection of Egyptian antiquities in the world. It is also considered by scholars and Egyptologists that in point of arrangement and classification of the objects collected here the Museum may serve as a model to most of the great museums of Europe. Then its scientific value is greatly enhanced by the fact that the place of origin of most of the antiquities is well known and generally indicated by labels. As a preliminary to the study of Egyptology, or even for an intelligent understanding of the monuments of the Upper Nile, a course of visits here is almost indispensable.

Since 1892 the Museum has been enlarged and the exhibits are arranged, for the most part, according to chronological order.

The following summary of the principal objects is taken from the latest edition (1896) of the Official Catalogue :—

In the garden is a huge marble sarcophagus containing the body of Mariette Pasha, the founder of the Museum.

Room I. 6. Statues of Ra-Hetep and his wife Nefert, found near the so-called False Pyramid of Medum. Fourth Dynasty.

Room II. 18. Stone statue of Ra-nefer. Considered one of the best specimens of sixth-dynasty sculpture yet discovered. From Sakkarah.

19. The famous wooden statue, popularly known as "The Village Sheik." This was discovered by Mariette at Sakkarah. This is a portrait statue "which possesses," writes Dr. Wallis Budge, "the greatest possible fidelity to life, and is a startling example of what the ancient Egyptian artist could attain to when he shook off the fetters of conventionality."

Room V. 64. Green diorite statue of Khephren, the builder of the Second Pyramid. He is represented seated on a throne which is decorated with the papyrus and lotus intertwined, which symbolises the union of Upper and Lower Egypt. On the pedestal is inscribed, "The image of the golden Horus, Khephren, beautiful god, lord of diadems." Dr. Wallis Budge, who has written the most complete and most intelligible popular account of the Museum of any hitherto published, considers this statue "one of the most remarkable pieces of Egyptian sculpture extant." Found in a well in the granite temple at Ghizeh (popularly known as the Temple of the Sphinx).

Room VII. 77. Limestone statue of Ti. Found in his tomb at Sakkarah. Fifth Dynasty.

Room X. This salon contains royal mummies of the Fifth and Sixth Dynasties.

107. Some *membra disjecta* of the mummy of King Oonas, which are quaintly labelled with a touch of grim humour, "Fragments of King Oonas"! This was found in the Pyramid of Oonas at Sakkarah. It is probably the most ancient mummy in existence.

Rooms XI.–XIII. contain a collection of stelæ from Abydos and Thebes of little interest to the ordinary visitor.

Rooms XIV.–XVI. The most interesting object in these rooms is the celebrated Hyksos Sphinx in black granite (No. 134) found by Mariette at Tanis (Zoan) in 1863. This statue, with its Asiatic cast of feature, is considered by some Egyptologists to furnish a proof of the Turanian origin of the Hyksos or Shepherd Kings. It probably belongs to some period anterior to B.C. 2000.

Room XXIV. 155. A colossal granite model of the

Sacred Boat of the God Ptah. Discovered at Memphis by M. de Morgan in 1892.

Room XXVI. 185 and 186. Two colossal sandstone statues of Ptah, discovered at Memphis by M. de Morgan in 1892.

213. Famous triumphal stela of Thothmes III. Found at Karnak. Eighteenth dynasty.

Room XXVII. 218. The celebrated stela, popularly known as the Tablet of Sakkarah, discovered by Mariette at Sakkarah in 1860. This stela is of the greatest value to chronologists and Egyptologists, as it gives the complete list of the names, with dates, of fifty-six of the early kings. It should be compared with the list in the Tablet of Abydos. The list begins with Merbapen, the sixth king of the first dynasty (instead of with Mena), and ends with Rameses II.

Rooms XXXIX. and XLV. are devoted to Græco-Roman antiquities. This collection is not a very representative one, and is not likely to be added to, as in future all discoveries of this period will be sent to the Græco-Roman Museum at Alexandria.

Room XL. 290. White limestone stela generally known as the "Stela of Canopus." It is inscribed in hieroglyphics, Demotic and Greek, with a decree made at Canopus by the priesthood assembled there from all parts of Egypt in honour of Ptolemy III. (Euergetes I.) There is a replica of this tablet in the Louvre. Probably had not the Rosetta Stone been first found, this tablet with its threefold inscription would have proved the key to the language and writing of the ancient Egyptians.

Room XLIX. The chief objects of interest in this room are the famous Tell el-Amarna Tablets. These are a portion of a collection of about 320 documents which were found at Tell el-Amarna, the site of the town built by Khu-en-aten, or Amenophis IV., which is situated about 180 miles south of Memphis. The Berlin Museum acquired 160, a large number being fragments, the British Museum 82, and the Ghizeh Museum 55. These documents were probably written between the years B.C. 1500-1450.

Rooms LVII. and LXII. contain papyri, chiefly historical. The collection of papyri in this Museum is, however, far inferior in value to those in many continental museums—Turin, Paris, and Berlin, for instance.

Room LXIII. Here is exhibited a very complete collection of amulets.

Room LXX. Beautiful collection of jewels belonging to Queen Aah-Hetep, the wife of Seqenen-Ra, found in the coffin of the Queen at Drah abul Nekka in 1860.

The collection of jewellery discovered at Dahshur by M. de Morgan in 1894 and 1895 is, however, still more valuable. The ornaments belonged to the Princesses Hathor-Sat and Ita of the twelfth dynasty, and consist of necklaces, bracelets, pectorals, amulets, clasps, etc., of exquisite workmanship. Among the most beautiful objects of the earlier "find" is a model in gold of the sacred bark of the dead with Amasis I. seated in the stern. The rowers are of silver, the chariot of wood and bronze. Another very interesting object is a gold head-dress inlaid with precious stones.

Room LXXI. contains a collection of Scarabs. "Scarab or scarabæus (from the Greek σκάραβος) is the name given by Egyptologists to the myriads of models of a certain beetle, which are found in mummies and tombs and in the ruins of temples and other buildings in Egypt, and in other countries, the inhabitants of which, from a remote period, had intercourse with the Egyptians."

These Scarabs were used as amulets, as ornaments, signet-rings, etc. The collection is considered a poor one by experts, and is certainly less historically valuable than collections in many European museums.

Room LXXIII. A collection of Egyptian flora.

Room LXXIV. At present this room is closed. It is intended to exhibit here a collection of Egyptian minerals.

Rooms LXXXV. and LXXXVI. These contain the mummies of the Priests of Amen, found in the royal necropolis of Dar-el-Bahari, near Thebes, in 1891.

Most visitors will, however, consider the most interesting objects in the whole of the Museum are the mummies of the ancient sovereigns of Egypt of the seventeenth, eighteenth, and nineteenth dynasties (about 1700 to 1100 B.C.), which were discovered by Brugsch Bey in 1881 at Dar-el-Bahari near Thebes,—one of the most important discoveries in the whole history of Egyptological research.

The most unimaginative tourist can scarcely help being impressed at beholding the *actual features* of the Pharoah of the Oppression, now brought to light after a period of some three thousand years. These mummies, officially known as the Dah-el-Bahari mummies, are to be seen in Room LXXXIV. The most important are:—

1174. Mummy of Seqenen-Ra. This king was killed in battle, and the features are terribly disfigured.

1175. Mummy of Amasis I.

1188 (*a*). Mummy of Thothmes II.

1180. Mummy of Seti I.

1181. MUMMY OF RAMESES II. ("the Pharaoh of the Oppression").

1182. Mummy of Rameses III.

1198. Coffin and Mummies of Queen Maat-ka-Ra (daughter of King Pa-seb-kha-nut) and her infant daughter Mut-em-hut. It is supposed that the Queen died in giving birth to her daughter.

Of the recent acquisitions the most interesting is the black granite stela which was discovered by Professor Petrie at Thebes in 1896. It is a kind of palimpsest inscription, for there are signs of erasures of an earlier inscription by Amen-Hetep III. (B.C. 1500) under one by Seti I. (Mer-en-Ptah). This stela is of the greatest importance to biblical students, as on the back of the stone is a long description describing the wars of the king with the Libyans and Syrians, in which occurs the phrase,

"The people of Israel is spoiled: it hath no seed." This is *the first allusion to the Israelites* by name found as yet on any Egyptian monument, whether Babylonian, Assyrian, or Egyptian.

Arab Museum.—Just as a visit to the monuments of Upper Egypt should be supplemented by a visit to the matchless collection of antiquities enshrined in the Ghizeh Palace, so it is essential, for a right understanding and appreciation of mediæval Saracenic art, to visit the Museum of Arabian Art in connection with the exploration of the Mosques. The museum is in a temporary building in the courtyard of the Mosque El-Hakim, and consists chiefly of objects of artistic or antiquarian interest collected from ruined mosques or rescued from the hands of the dealers in antiquities, who for years, with the cognisance of the guardians, had been pillaging some of the ruined mosques. The Museum was mainly due to the zeal of the late Rogers Bey, and Franz Pasha, formerly director under the Wakfs Administration. In its temporary home the collection is rather cramped, and the Government have recently voted a sum of £32,000 for a special building, the foundation stone of which was laid in the spring of the present year (1897).

The most beautiful and characteristic objects will be found in rooms three and five. In the first salon is the incomparable collection of enamelled mosque lamps. Most of these have been taken from the mosques, especially Sultan Hassan. The date of these lamps is of the thirteenth, fourteenth, and fifteenth centuries, but their place of manufacture is unknown. The earlier of these lamps, which constitute the chief glory of the Museum, are in the purest style of Arabic decoration, though probably the fifteenth century ones are not indigenous but imported from Murano. Scarcely a hundred of these lamps are extant, and most are to be found in this unique collection. In rooms five and seven is a large and representative collection of mushrabiyeh (lattice-work) and mosaic woodwork. Other rooms contain specimens of metal-work, faience, stucco, pottery, etc.

"In one essential respect this museum," says Mr. Stanley Lane-Poole, "differs from others. The objects here are relative and were not designed as separate works of art. They are, in fact, dependent upon the monuments to which they once belonged." Most of the objects consist of portions of the decoration and furniture of mosques and private houses. This, of course, makes it the more regrettable that, owing to the neglect of the mosques, they cannot be seen *in situ*, where they would be more in harmony with their environment.

IX.—THE CITADEL

THIS mediæval fortress is one of the most interesting of the historic buildings of the Egyptian capital, and is one of its most striking landmarks. It was built by Saladin, though the name of its founder is apt to be over-shadowed in the minds of visitors by the dominant personality of Mehemet Ali, who, however, only restored the walls. The memory of this oriental Napoleon is certainly closely associated with the principal historical events of the fortress.

This Cairene acropolis is, like the Kremlin or the Alhambra, a town within a town, and contains, besides several mosques, a palace (now used as officers' quarters), hospital, prison, barracks, arsenal, etc., within its walls.

The usual entrance to the citadel is through the Bab-el-Azab, a gateway which is a fine specimen of Saracenic architecture, and along a steep and narrow road between high walls. It was here that the terrible massacre of the Mameluke Beys by Mehemet

Ali in 1811 took place. This crime is the great blot of Mehemet's reign, though it may, perhaps, be urged in extenuation that the existence of this rebellious element imperilled the Sultan's personal safety, and that the peace of Egypt was as much endangered by the Mamelukes as was that of the Porte by the Janissaries a few years later, when a similar atrocity was perpetrated.

The Bey's Leap.—In the opinion of the guides the most interesting site is the spot on the eastern terrace known as the Bey's Leap, where it is said that Emin Bey made his legendary leap over the battlements to escape the slaughter.

"The Beys came, mounted on their finest horses, in magnificent uniforms, forming the most superb cavalry in the world. After a very flattering reception from the Pasha, they were requested to parade in the court of the Citadel.

"They entered the fortification unsuspectingly—the portcullis fell behind the last of the proud procession, a moment's glance revealed to them their doom. They dashed forwards — in vain! before, behind, around them nothing was visible but blank pitiless walls and barred windows; the only opening was towards the bright blue sky, even that was soon darkened by their funeral pile of smoke, as volley after volley flashed from a thousand muskets behind the ramparts upon this defenceless and devoted band. Startling and fearfully sudden as was their death, they met it as became their fearless character—some with arms crossed upon their mailed bosoms, and turbaned heads devoutly bowed in prayer, some with flashing swords and fierce curses, alike unavailing against their dastard and ruthless foe. All that chivalrous and splendid throng save one sank rapidly beneath the deadly fire into a red and writhing mass—that one was Emin Bey. He spurred his charger over a heap of his slaughtered comrades, and sprang upon the battlements. It was a dizzy height, but the next moment he was in the air—another, and he was disengaging himself from his crushed and dying horse amid a shower of bullets. He escaped, and found safety in the sanctuary of a mosque, and ultimately in the deserts of the Thebaid."

Thus Warburton graphically describes the Bey's remarkable escape from this treacherous massacre. It is a pity to spoil such a thrilling and dramatic story, but there is little doubt that this remarkable feat of horsemanship is purely mythical. The Bey, as a matter of fact, wisely absented himself from this grim *levée* of his Sultan. He had been warned at the last moment, and fled into Syria.

There are several mosques within the walls of the citadel, but with the exception of the Mosque

Mohammed Nasr and the Mosque Sulieman Pasha they are modern and of the Constantinople pattern.

Mosque of Mehemet Ali.—This beautiful mosque, often called the Alabaster Mosque, was built, it is said, in a spirit of cynicism by the grim old Sultan on the very threshold of the scene of the massacre of the Mamelukes. The proportions are imposing, and the interior is richly decorated, but architects hold it in little esteem as being an inferior copy of the Mosque Nasr Osmaniya at Constantinople. The minarets, however, are lofty and elegant. This is one of the show-mosques of Cairo, in spite of its artistic shortcomings, and owes, perhaps, its popularity to its size, noble situation, and as the burial place of Mehemet Ali.

Mosque of Mohammed Nasr.—This is usually called the Old Mosque to distinguish it from the Mosque of Mehemet Ali. It was built by this Sultan (son of the Sultan Kalaun) in 1318, a few years later than the Nasr Mohammed Mosque next to the Muristan. This was formerly considered the Royal Mosque, but for many years it has been laicised and used as a military prison and store-house. Thanks to the exertions of the Society for the Preservation of Arabic Monuments, it has within recent years been restored and can now be seen by visitors. It is, however, not now used as a place of worship, and is, in fact, usually closed, but the key can be obtained at the lodge at the entrance to the citadel. The arcaded kibla is beautifully ornamented with rich arabesques.

Mosque of Sulieman Pasha.—This is built on the walls of the citadel, and is interesting, though of an inferior and late style of architecture, chiefly Byzantine in character. It was built by Sultan Selim, the Ottoman conqueror of Egypt, who was formerly known as Sulieman Pasha. The interior is lavishly decorated. In general appearance the mosque resembles Saint Sophia of Constantinople.

Joseph's Well.—This is a shaft of vast proportions and great depth cut through the solid rock to a depth of nearly 300 feet. It has, it need hardly be said, no connection with the Hebrew patriarch, to whom it is attributed by the guides. It is named after Saladin, whose Arabic name was Yusuf (Joseph), who either excavated or, as is generally held by antiquarians, opened up an old well dug by the ancient Egyptians. Visitors can descend by a kind of spiral roadway, and the well is quite worth a close examination (fee 2 p.). It is supposed that the bottom of the well is on the same level as the Nile. It is not now much used, as since 1866 the citadel has been supplied with water by the Cairo Water Company.

View from the Terrace.—The prospect from the

southern ramparts is justly famous, and may be included among the world's most famous points of view. The citadel is worth visiting at sunset for the view alone.

X.—THE TOMBS OF THE CALIPHS

THOUGH some of the best specimens of Saracenic architecture are to be found among this congeries of dilapidated tomb-mosques, which form such a striking landmark in all views of Cairo, they are not likely to prove very attractive to the ordinary tourist. For one thing, most are in ruins, and hitherto the Wakfs Administration, perhaps feeling that the intra-mural mosques, being still used for public worship, had stronger claims, have done little in the work of restoration.

The ordinary visitor will probably be satisfied with an inspection of the best preserved mosques—Kait Bey, Barkuk, and El-Ashraf. But those fond of architecture are recommended to inspect carefully the exterior of many of the less known tomb-mosques. The interiors are rarely worth visiting, and in many cases strangers will feel that they are intruders, as some of the ruined mosques afford a refuge for homeless Arabs and their families, who "squat" here unmolested, like gipsies. The Tombs of the Caliphs are easily reached, as they are only a short distance beyond the walls at the end of the Rue Neuve. Hurried tourists can conveniently combine this excursion with a visit to the Cairo Mosques of Mohammedan-Nasr, Barkukiya, Muristan Kalaun, El-Ghuri, El-Ashraf, and El-Azhar.

Tourists, indeed, with little time to spare will find that an economy of space means economy of time even more in Cairo than other oriental cities.

These tombs have no connection with the Caliphs, but the misnomer has been so long in use that it is idle to expect the guides and donkey-boys to employ a more accurate designation, though the Tombs are occasionally known as the Cemetery of Kait Bey from the principal mosque. The Cairene Caliphs have, indeed, no separate burial place, and the Sultans who are buried here belonged to the Circassian Mameluke dynasty, and most of the mosques date from the fifteenth century.

The term Caliph is, indeed, rather loosely used in connection with the history of Saracen rule in Egypt. The Mameluke Sultans were not strictly Caliphs, in the sense of spiritual head of Islam, and orthodox Mohammedans regarded the representatives of the Abbaside dynasty, overthrown by Ibn Tulun, as Caliphs *de jure.* The Baharide and Circassian

Mameluke Sultans were merely Caliphs *de facto*. Indeed, most of these Sultans, with the view of conciliating the orthodox Moslems, formally recognised the claims of the descendants of the Abbasides as spiritual successors of Mohammed. In fact, the present Sultan of Turkey claims to have inherited the title of Caliph through the last scion of the Abbaside Caliphs, who died at Constantinople in 1538, some twenty years after the Conquest of Egypt by the Porte. After his death each successive Sultan assumed the title of Caliph.

Mosque of Kait Bey.—The elegant dome of the Kait Bey Mosque is its most distinctive feature. Few among the innumerable mosques of Cairo can rival this beautiful exterior, for unlike most mosques, the architectural embellishments are lavished on the exterior, and the interior is comparatively unadorned. "Looked at externally or internally," says Fergusson, "nothing can exceed the grace of every part of this building. Its small dimensions exclude it from any claim of grandeur, nor does it pretend to the purity of the Greek and some other styles; but as a perfect model of the elegance we generally associate with the architecture of this people, it is, perhaps, unrivalled by anything in Egypt, and far surpasses the Alhambra, or the western buildings of its age."

Two sacred relics are shown by the guides, viz.

two slabs of red and black granite, in one of which is a depression of the size of a man's foot. Needless to say, a legend attaches to these stones which are said to have been brought from Mecca, and the depression is said to be the impress of Mohammed's foot.

Mosque of Barkuk.—At the other extremity of the cemetery is the large and imposing Mosque of Barkuk, easily recognised by its fine twin domes and twin minarets. In fact, this mosque is a double one, and each dome marks respectively the burial place of the male and female members of Sultan Barkuk, the first of the Circassian Mameluke dynasty. This style of architecture is not common among the Cairene mosques. A great portion of the building is in ruins, but the remains give the spectator an idea of its magnificent proportions. The symmetrical plan of the edifice, its massive masonry, and the symmetrical disposition of the rows of pilasters with domes, makes this mosque one of the most perfect examples of Arabian architecture in existence. Very picturesque cloisters and a beautifully chased stone pulpit are some of the more noticeable features of this building. The Sultan is buried under the north dome, and a stone column hard by will be shown by the guide. It is said to be of the same height as the deceased Sultan. This mosque was built by a son of Barkuk early in the fifteenth century. It must not be confounded with the Barkuk Mosque, next the Kalaun Mosque, which was built by the Sultan himself.

El-Ashraf.—This is the mosque of the Sultan Bursbey (in full El-Ashraf Bursbey). In spite of a stormy career, this ruler earned the unusual distinction of dying a natural death (1438). The dome with its intricate pattern of stone-chasing is very striking, and a mosaic pavement in coloured stones is an excellent specimen of Saracenic art.

The above are the show-mosques, but there are many others, some of unknown origin, scattered about this extensive necropolis which, at all events, make excellent subjects for sketches.

The extensive Mohammedan cemetery, which extends almost from the Tombs of the Caliphs to the walls of Cairo, contains nothing worth visiting except the tomb (recently restored) of the oriental explorer, Burckhardt, who died at Cairo in 1817. This famous traveller, like the unfortunate Professor Palmer, is preserved in the memories of the Arabs under a native name, Sheik Ibrahim.

The Tombs of the Mamelukes.—The mosque-tombs of these Sultans, who belonged to the dynasty of the Baharide Mamelukes (1250-1376 A.D.), immediately preceding that of the Circassian Mamelukes ("Tombs of the Caliphs"), stand in a cluster a little south of the citadel. They are in an even more ruinous state than the Tombs of the Caliphs, and very little is known of the builders, as there has been no systematic examination of the ruins. In fact, in Egypt purely Saracenic monuments have been entirely ignored by antiquarians, who seem to despise all remains of a later date than the Ptolemies. This necropolis may be regarded as a kind of whited sepulchre, for the view at a distance of the lofty and elegant minarets and domes does not prepare the visitor for the scanty ruins, in most cases the mere outer shell of a mosque, which a close inspection reveals.

The fact that these tomb-mosques are more than a century older than those in the Kait Bey Cemetery is no doubt partly accountable for their more ruinous condition. They are easily reached by the Bab El-Karafeh beyond the Place Mehemet Ali.

The mosque nearest the Gebel Mokattam will interest students of Saracenic architecture on account of its curious double dome—one within the other—a form seldom seen in Egyptian mosques.

A little south of the tombs of the Mamelukes is the curious tomb-mosque of the Imam-esh-Shafih. This cannot, however, be visited without a special order from the Wakfs Administration, not easily obtained. Close by are the mausolea containing the tombs of Thewfik and various members of the Khedivial family.

XI.—OLD CAIRO AND RODA ISLAND

OLD Cairo, for modern Cairo, *i.e.* Cairo within the walls, is for Egypt a mere *parvenu* city, dating only from the tenth century, lies about three miles south of the citadel, between the Tombs of the Mamelukes and the Island of Roda. It is the site of the camp of Amru (A.D. 638), the general of the Caliph Omar, and was then called Fostat. Large mounds of rubbish, which might, one would imagine, repay systematic excavation, occupy a great portion of the site of Amru's encampment.

The principal places to be visited in this excursion are the Mosque of Amru, the Aqueduct of Saladin, the Coptic and Greek Churches, and, in the Isle of Roda, the Nilometer.

Formerly Old Cairo was not very easy of access, but now, by means of the new electric tramway, which runs from Esbekiyeh Square to the head of the Khalig (opposite Roda Island), it is quickly and conveniently reached. By this means the various sights mentioned above, with a superficial inspection of some of the Coptic churches and convents, can be managed in one morning.

A. J. Butler's *Ancient Coptic Churches* (see "Bibliography") will be found an indispensable companion for the visitor desirous of thoroughly inspecting these remarkably interesting buildings.

Mosque of Amru.—This is called the oldest mosque in Cairo, but it is so in a very restricted sense, as there are very few remains of the ancient mosque built by Amru. The greater part of the present mosque is of fourteenth-century architecture. In the rebuilding and frequent restoration the original design—a city of the Kaaba at Mecca—has, however, been preserved, and some of the ancient materials were built into the walls.

This mosque is still held in the greatest veneration by the Cairenes, who call it the "Crown of Mosques." The late Khedive Thewfik contemplated its thorough restoration, but very little has been done, and it remains in a very decayed state. The chief curiosity is a column (close to the Mimbar) which the devout believe to have been miraculously transported by the Caliph Omar from Mecca to Cairo at the request of his general, Amru. There is a curious legend in connection with this column. According to the tradition the column first disobeyed the command of the Caliph to betake itself to Cairo, whereupon he struck it with his whip (*kurbash*). In proof whereof the guide will show an outline of the whip in the veining of the marble.

Next to the miraculous column the chief objects of interest, in the estimation of the guides, are a pair of columns between which a man could barely squeeze. These are known as the "Needle's Eye," and the tradition is that this feat can only be performed by men of the highest integrity. These columns have, however, been recently walled up. In fact it is said that the space was filled up by Ismail's orders, as he saw at a glance that his portly form could not stand the test!

Just as the Mosque of Sultan Hassan ranks as the great mosque of the State, this ancient foundation of Amru is regarded by Cairenes as peculiarly the mother-church of Cairo, and a prophecy, implicitly believed by devout Moslems, predicts the downfall of Moslem power whenever this mosque shall fall to decay. It is here that the universal service of supplication is held, when a tardy or insufficient rising of the Nile takes place, a service attended by the Khedive and the principal officers of State.

The gloomy interior with its forest of pillars—over 200 in number—many spoils from the temple of Memphis and Heliopolis, resembles that of the El-

Azhar Mosque. These pillars support rows of arches in the colonnades which bound each side of an open court, for the general design—a square court surrounded by colonnades—is similar to that of the Mosque of Tulun. A striking and unique architectural feature is the pointed arch which, according to some authorities, is the earliest prototype of the Norman arch. Fergusson, however, considers that the pointed arches are of later date than the round ones adjoining them.

Roman Fortress.—This stronghold once covered a wide area, but hardly any traces remain of this ancient fortress—the scanty ruins of its walls, which can be safely identified, being incorporated with the Coptic churches in the Der (Fort) Mari Girghis (or Kasr-es-Shemma) which occupies the site of the ancient Roman castle. A peculiarity of these Coptic and Greek churches is that they are mostly enclosed within a walled enclosure called Der. There are many of these Ders in Old Cairo which serve the purpose of fortified precincts, often comprising, besides churches and convents, schools, dwelling-houses, shops, etc. With the exception of Abou Sergeh (generally called St. Mary's Church) and the Greek Church of St. George, they are little known to visitors, or, for the matter of that, to the European residents, yet their high architectural importance, and the valuable works of art they often contain, invite careful inspection. The comparative neglect of these early Christian churches on the part of travellers is partly due to the ignorance of the dragomans and guides, whose knowledge of the ecclesiastical buildings of Old Cairo is as a rule confined to the Mosque of Amru, the Church of St. Mary, and the Greek convent. It is therefore the best plan to dispense with the ordinary Cairo guide and engage a Coptic one on the spot.

There are nearly a dozen Coptic churches in Old Cairo, but, except to those who take a special interest in ecclesiastical architecture and art, a visit to those mentioned above and the churches of Abou Sephin and El-Adra, both situated within the walls of the old Roman citadel, will probably suffice. These are certainly the most interesting.

The exterior is usually characterised by a marked simplicity and absence of decoration; and, with the windows looking like loop-holes, a Coptic church somewhat resembles a fort, and the Byzantine influence is clearly traceable in the basilica form.

The internal arrangements approximate more nearly to those of a Greek church than a Roman Catholic or Protestant one. The body of the church is divided into three compartments, the first is a kind of vestibule, the second is set apart for women, and the third, next the choir, for men. East of the chancel is the *hekel*, or sanctuary, and behind this again the apse, with the episcopal throne. The ritual in some respects resembles that of the Greek Church ; there is no organ, the only instruments being cymbals and brass bells struck with a rod. "There are no images, but a number of paintings in the stiff Byzantine style, some of them not wanting in a kind of rude grandeur." The above-mentioned churches are all, with the exception of Abou Sephin, in the Der of the ruined Roman castle.

El-Adra.—This is often known as the "Hanging Church," as it is built on the top of one of the ruined towers. It has been recently restored, and many of the decorations have unfortunately been removed to the Coptic rooms in the Ghizeh Museum. Some exquisitely carved panels are now in the British Museum. The things best worth inspection are the *hekel* (chancel) screen and the beautifully sculptured pulpit.

Abou Sirgeh.—This is the prototype of the ancient Coptic churches. Its style may be described as Egypto-Byzantine. The crypt is the oldest portion of the building, and probably dates from the sixth century. The Copts hand down the tradition that the Virgin Mary concealed herself and her Child in this crypt after her flight to Egypt, and this crypt is dedicated to Sitt Miriam (the Lady Mary).

Abou Sephin. — This remarkably interesting church is in the Der of the same name. Fortunately all the beautiful wood-carvings, mosaics, screens, and other decorations have been allowed to remain. The most venerated object is the mummified arm of St. Macarius. Near the well or font is a curious stone column, of unknown date, with an Arabic inscription.

Roda Island.—A visit to Roda Island and the famous Nilometer being generally combined with the excursion to Old Cairo, a short description of this beautiful island may be conveniently given here. The island is a pretty and shady retreat covered with groves and gardens. An Arabic tradition has chosen a certain part of the shore opposite the Hospital of Kasr-el-Aini as the site of the finding of Moses by Pharaoh's daughter. The spot is marked by a tall palm, with an unusually smooth trunk which is called Moses' Tree.

The Nilometer (the column used to mark the rise of the Nile) is the chief object of interest in the island, and is situated at the southern end, exactly opposite the site of the old Roman fortress of Babylon, and consists of a column about thirty feet high, which is erected at the bottom of a well-like chamber crowned by a modern dome roof, which has direct communication with the Nile. Owing to the elevation of the river-bed the traditional height of sixteen cubits (about twenty-eight feet) on the column, when the cutting of the banks of the irrigation canals is permitted, does not actually mean a rise of the Nile to this extent. At Cairo a rise of twenty-six feet is considered a good average.

In former times the taxation of the fellahs was arranged on a sliding scale dependent on the rise of the Nile. It need scarcely be said, when we remember the fiscal methods of the Egyptian Government, even as recently as the time of the Khedive Ismail, that this custom gave rise to much dishonesty on the part of the officials who had the custody of the Nilometer, and they invariably proclaimed the rise to be greater than it actually was.

The rise of the Nile, and the consequent ceremony of cutting the dam of the Khalig Canal, is celebrated by an important festival. It is not a poetical metaphor, but an actual fact, that the Nile is the one beneficent Providence of Egypt, and therefore it is not surprising, that as a period of universal rejoicing, the Khalig Fête outshines many of the great religious festivals. The ceremony is rarely witnessed by tourists, as it usually takes place in the beginning of August. If the improvements promised by the Egyptian Government are carried out, one of the most picturesque and characteristic of Cairene festivals will probably be abolished, or degenerate into a meaningless ceremony, as by the drainage of the Khalig its *raison d'être* will be destroyed, for, as already mentioned, the intention is to convert the ancient water-way—in the early summer virtually an open sewer—into a tramway.

Aqueduct.—The ruined aqueduct near the mouth of the Khalig is a very picturesque feature, and though the guide-books are inclined to ignore it, it is quite worth a visit. The local guides ascribe it to Saladin, but it was actually built by the Sultan Ghuri.

It was intended to supply the citadel with water from the Nile, and though now in a ruinous condition, traces of the grand workmanship can still be recognised. The length is about two and a quarter miles, and the water was conducted by seven stages, being raised from one level to the other by Sakyehs. The southern end terminates in a massive square tower over two hundred feet high. The summit can be conveniently reached by a gently inclined pathway, similar to the one at Joseph's well in the Citadel. The view from the top is very striking. Those who intend visiting the Coptic churches, will find it a convenient way of making acquaintance with the puzzling topography of the Coptic quarter.

XII.—MINOR SIGHTS

The principal places of interest in Cairo have now, it is hoped, been described in sufficient detail, but when the visitor has exhausted the regulation sights, he will find that there is still plenty to be seen, and that to know Cairo properly means even more than a winter's study. The Government and other public buildings of Cairo are, with the exception of the Public Library, scarcely worth visiting. It is true that some of the numerous Khedivial Palaces—and the Khedive Ismail, who is responsible for some half a dozen, seems to have had almost as pronounced a mania for building costly and unnecessary palaces, as the late King Ludwig of Bavaria—are on the programme of most of the guides, but these are only worth visiting on account of the beautiful gardens attached to them, notably in the case of Ghezireh (now an hotel) and Shubra Palaces.

The Public Library.—This is open daily (except Friday) and admission is free. It is situated next the Ministry of Education in the Darb-el-Gamamiz. It contains a fine collection of illuminated copies of the Koran, probably the best collection in existence. One of these, which is written in Kufic characters, is said to be the work of scribes of 1200 years ago. The most valuable books and MSS. in many of the Mosque libraries have been removed to this national library, which contains some 25,000 volumes. The books can be consulted by students if furnished with a consular letter of recommendation.

Port of Cairo. — The artist as well as the ordinary tourist should not omit a stroll along the Boulaq quays. This emporium of all the commerce of Upper Egypt and Nubia is a particularly lively scene, and a colourist would revel in the pictures of native life and the variety of form and colour. Strangers hardly realise that Cairo has an important trading-port at its gates, and certainly no guide would think of suggesting the inclusion of Boulaq in the traveller's daily round of sight-seeing.

Montbard's graphic description gives a good idea of what the observant visitor will see, though, of course, since the closing of the Soudan to traders—soon no doubt to be re-opened — cargoes from Khartoum or Upper Nubia are no longer to be seen.

"Dahabeahs with elevated poops advance: they hail from Esneh with ivory and ostrich feathers;

coffee and incense from Arabia; spice, pearls, precious stones, cashmeres and silk from India arriving by the deserts of Kosseir. Edfu sends its pipes, its charming vases in red and black clay, elegant in form, with gracefully modelled ornaments. And there are heavy barges from Fayyoum, the land of roses, filled to the top with rye, barley, cotton, indigo; dahabiyehs full of carpets, woollen stuffs, flagons of rose-water, and mats made with the reeds of Birket-el-Keroun."

Mohammedan Festivals.—If the visitor is anxious to get some insight into the life of the people, he should make a point of attending some of the public festivals. These religious fêtes offer a better field for the study of Cairene native life than continuous visits to the region of the bazaars.

The year being lunar, the dates of the festivals vary annually, any particular fête running through all the seasons in the course of thirty-three years. The principal are the Anniversary of the Death of Hassein, Departure of the Pilgrims for Mecca, Birthday (Molid) of Mahomet, the Night of the Record, and the Great Beiram.

If the date of the commencement of the Moslem year is known, the exact date of any particular festival is easily arrived at, for each month consists of twenty-eight days. For instance, the Mohammedan year 1315, corresponding to 1897 A.D., began on 2nd June. During the season 1897-98, strangers will be able to see something of the national fêtes described below.

The most characteristic of all is the Molid of Mahomet, a great national holiday. But unfortunately, for the next few years this will fall in August or September, when Egypt is, of course, deserted by tourists.

Night of the Ascension to Paradise.—This is celebrated in the last week of December. Many of the mosques are lit up with coloured lamps, and special performances of the dancing dervishes take place in the Place Abdin, which is brilliantly illuminated in the evening.

The Night of the Shaaban (sometimes called "Night of the Record"). This takes place on the 14th of Shaaban, the eighth month, which begins on the 26th December. This is the most solemn night in the whole Mohammedan year, when, according to immemorial custom, the Khedive pays his devotions in the Mosque of Mehemet Ali. The belief is that on this night the Sidr, the lotus-tree which bears as many leaves as there are human beings, is shaken by an angel in Paradise, and on each leaf that falls is inscribed the name of some person who will infallibly die before the end of the year. Naturally, a strong personal interest is behind the prayers and intercessions made to Allah and Mahomet on this night, and it is not surprising that the Mosques are thronged.

The next month, that of Ramadan (begins 24th January) is peculiarly the sacred month of the Moslem year, and many important festivals take place. On the 13th of this month, the Mosque of Mehemet Ali is brilliantly lit up, and long extracts from the Koran are read before his tomb. The Khedive and his household are sometimes present. In other portions of the mosque *zikrs* (religious exercises) of the Howling and Twirling Dervishes take place.

Procession of the Mecca Pilgrims.—Strangers who are in Cairo in April, should not omit seeing this interesting spectacle, which is the occasion of one of the most striking and characteristic of the many Cairene festivals. It takes place some time in the third week of April. The best place to view the cavalcade is from the Place Mehemet Ali below the Citadel. The chief feature in the procession is the *Mahmal*, a kind of litter in the form of a baldacchino, which is borne on a richly-caparisoned camel at the head of the procession of pilgrims, who are preceded by detachments of cavalry and bands of music.

The most superstitious reverence is paid to this canopy by the populace of all classes, and the Khedive and his Officers of State are usually present.

The more popular celebrations, as distinct from the religious services in the mosques, of these Molids and other Cairene festivals, what the natives would call a *Fantasia*—a comprehensive word meaning spectacle, or treat, or anything in the nature of holiday-making—generally take place outside the city on the borders of the desert, or on some open space outside the walls. Here the religious elements of the anniversary are not unduly prominent. The spectacle of the encampment is striking and even picturesque to European eyes. It reminds the English visitor of a country fair in an oriental setting. There are streets of tents and booths, with swings and roundabouts, while troupes of mountebanks, itinerant musicians, jugglers, story-tellers, snake-charmers, etc., form rings among the surging crowds of holiday-makers, and keep up a continuous round of performances all day and the greater part of the night. In another part of the ground the fanatical dances and posturings of bands of dervishes will attract crowded audiences of interested spectators. At night the pavilions and tents are all lit up, and a display of fireworks brings the spectacular portion of the festival to an end, though the droning of the readers of the Koran and the mad dances of the dervishes will go on almost uninterruptedly till dawn.

Howling and Twirling Dervishes.—The religious exercises of these fanatical orders are decidedly repulsive spectacles, but as they are among the recognized sights of Cairo—in fact to enable strangers to witness the spectacle (which usually begins at 2 P.M.) the *table-d'hôte* lunch at the chief hotels takes place an hour earlier than usual—it is necessary to notice them. Performances of the Howling Dervishes take place every Friday in the Mosque of Kasr-el-Ain, a few minutes' walk from the mouth of the Khalig. The performances, called *zikrs,* though decidedly repulsive to western tastes, are tame and perfunctory compared to the *zikrs* at the great festivals described above.

The beginning is comparatively sober and restrained, the performers, who stand in a circle, slowly bending their heads to and fro in unison, while ejaculating invocation to Allah in a peculiar kind of grunt. Gradually the swaying becomes more violent, the body being bent alternately backwards and forwards, the shaggy black manes of the dervishes sweeping the ground. The groaning and grunting gets louder, and the pace of the backward and forward motions succeed each other so rapidly as to make some spectators giddy. Occasionally, some of the more excitable fanatics will fall on the floor in a paroxysm of ecstatic emotion, which is perhaps only partially factitious, and has all the appearance, at least, of a genuine epileptic fit. At this point ladies, who are usually well represented among the spectators, will be well advised to retire. A baksheesh of a least four piastres is expected from strangers.

The Friday *zikrs* of the Twirling Dervishes take place in the Tekiyeh (Monastery) El-Akbar, near the Place Sultan Hassan. They have of late years been occasionally suspended, so tourists cannot always count upon seeing the spectacle. It is a less unpleasant performance to watch than that of their confrères, the "Howlers," but far more remarkable. It would not be beyond the powers of any robust Christian to groan, gasp, and sway the body by the hour together, but to revolve within a circle of three feet diameter, at the rate of sixty to seventy times a minute for over half an hour, is an accomplishment requiring a considerable amount of skill and muscular activity. Besides, one must allow a certain amount of religious fervour to these dervishes, which seems altogether wanting to the brutalising exercises of the Howling Dervishes. The striking performance has been well described by Mr. H. D. Traill :—

"The world of sight must long have disappeared from his view; the whizzing universe would be a mere blur upon his retina, were he to open his eyes. But does he see nothing beyond it through their closed lids? Has he really twirled himself in imagination to the Gates of Paradise? Perhaps the incessant rotatory movement acts on the human brain like hashish. This dervish, at any rate, has all the air of the wonder-seer. He is of the true race of the Visionaries, and even if he were not, the stupor of trance is, at any rate, a less unwholesome and distressing subject of contemplation than the spasms of epilepsy. The performance of the Twirling Dervish leaves no sense of a degraded humanity behind it; but you quit the company of their grunting and gasping brothers, with all the feeling of having assisted at a 'camp meeting' of the lower apes."

Other minor sights, which might perhaps be included among what Americans might call the "side-shows" of Cairo, are the native cafés, where dances by the Ghawazee girls are the chief attraction. They are, however, poor imitations of the dances that may be seen in the Upper Nile villages. They are lacking in local colour, and the performances are decidedly banal and vulgar.

Six Days' Itinerary.—Even those who have

only a few days for Cairo and its excursions, can see a good deal, with the minimum waste of time, by adopting the following itinerary:—

First Day (*Monday*).—Morning: Bazaars, and the Mosques near the Bazaar region (see chapter on "Mosques"). Afternoon: Tombs of the Caliphs and the Citadel.

Second Day (*Tuesday*).—Morning: Mosques and Arab Museum. Afternoon: Old Cairo (Coptic Churches, Mosque Amru, Aqueduct) and Roda Island (Nilometer).

Third Day (*Wednesday*).—Morning: National Museum. Afternoon: Heliopolis, Matarieh, and on return Koubbeh Palace (Station). Frequent trains.

Fourth Day (*Thursday*).—Morning: Barrage. Afternoon: Small Petrified Forest.

Fifth Day (*Friday*).—Morning: Pyramids. Afternoon: Dancing Dervishes and Twirling Dervishes. Khedivial Library. Tombs of the Mamelukes.

Sixth Day (*Saturday*).—Sakkarah.

What to Omit.—Those who have only a week to spare for Cairo and its sights and excursions should be proof to the persuasions of the guides, and omit the following excursions: the Palaces, Ostrich Farm, and Helouan; and devote the time saved to a more thorough examination of the Mosques, the Bazaars, or the Ghizeh Museum.

PART II

EXCURSIONS

I.—THE PYRAMIDS OF GHIZEH

Routes.—The usual way of "doing" the Pyramids is to take a cab from Cairo after an early breakfast, and return to Cairo in time for lunch. Fare 15s. or 16s. This includes two to three hours' stay, but only gives time for a climb to the summit of the Pyramid of Cheops, and a glance at the Sphinx, and possibly a hasty visit to the interior of the Great Pyramid. Such a hurried visit is, however, most unsatisfactory. A better way and not much more expensive is to hire a donkey at Cairo in the cool of the evening, and ride to the Mena House Hotel, at the foot of the Pyramids, to sleep. By this means the Pyramid can be climbed in comfort and comparative privacy early the next morning before the usual horde of tourists arrive from Cairo. Then one can return to Cairo by the Mena House Coach, which usually leaves after lunch. The total cost of this excursion need not exceed £1 : 5s. or £1 : 10s.

A very economical, as well as comfortable, method of doing the Pyramids, which can be recommended to the active tourist, is simply to hire a good donkey at Cairo for the day for twenty-five or thirty piastres, devote the morning to the ascent and interior of the Great Pyramid, then lunch at Mena House Hotel, and in the afternoon visit the Sphinx and other monuments in the Pyramid plateau. It should be observed, however, that for some reason, taking a donkey for the Pyramid excursion is considered by the Cairo guides and dragomans a decidedly heterodox method of doing the excursion, but the seasoned traveller is not likely to mind this.

It may be mentioned that Messrs. Cook will undertake this trip, providing a comfortable carriage and pair for a party of not less than three, at a charge of twelve shillings a head, which includes the fee to the Sheik of the Pyramids.

So much for the various methods of doing this trip. The visitor, even if he has only a few days to spare for Cairo, is strongly advised to give a whole day to the excursion, and a start should be made early in the morning, so as to finish the climb (which, though presenting no danger or difficulty, is extremely tedious) before the sun gets too hot. Of course the Pyramids can be done, and often are, in one morning, but in such a hurried excursion a great deal of the interest and pleasure usually afforded by the trip would be lost. There certainly would be no time to enjoy the magnificent view from the top. Tourists in Egypt seem often to enter upon the work—hard labour, indeed—of sight-seeing, as if anxious to emulate the feat of the Chicago millionaire, who used to boast that he had "done all the picture galleries of Europe in a fortnight."

The drive to the foot of the Great Pyramid, along a well-made road ten miles in length, and shaded with lebbek trees all the way, takes about an hour and a half.

The construction of the electric tramway extension from the Kasr-en-Nil Bridge to the Pyramids is making good progress, and it will probably be finished in the course of the winter of 1897-98.

Perhaps there is no ancient monument in existence which has been so much written about and which has formed the subject of so much controversy as the Great Pyramid. The wildest and most extravagant theories have been ventilated in an attempt to solve the meaning and account for the object of these remarkable structures.

Many writers, however, content themselves with attributing a merely symbolical origin to the pyramids. Perhaps the most original idea was that of a French *savant* who maintained that the Pyramids were built as a barrier to protect the cities on the banks of the Nile from sand-storms. Now, happily, the fables and speculations to which these structures have given rise are, for the most part, exploded. The overwhelming weight of evidence, the fruit of the exhaustive researches of trained observers and scientists, is in favour of their having simply been used as royal tombs.

Besides, the mere fact that each of the sixteen identified pyramids, out of the seventy in the great pyramid field which extends from Ghizeh to Medûm, is indisputably a tomb, should alone be a sufficient answer to these absurd speculations.

It is scarcely necessary to do more than recapitulate here the popular information about the Pyramids. Every Egyptian traveller is aware that these buildings were built by the sovereigns of the fourth dynasty, that they are probably the oldest monuments in tolerable preservation in Egypt, dating from a period so remote that almost as many centuries separate them from the famous temples of Abydos, Thebes, and Abou Simbel as separate these famous ruins from the great buildings of the Ptolemies. We all know that the pyramids were built of limestone from the Mokattam quarries on the other side of the Nile, and cased with polished granite slabs, which was laid under contribution after the Arab conquest to build the walls and mosques of Cairo.

Dimensions of the Great Pyramid.—According to the latest statistics (Petrie) the height is a little over 451 feet, and each side is 755 feet long at the base, and the area occupies 535,824 square feet. These statistics, however, convey little to the non-scientific visitor, and the enormous proportions of this huge monument are better realised if we remember the oft-quoted statement that the Pyramid occupies an area equal to that of Lincoln's Inn Fields, viz. thirteen acres. As to the bulk (85,000,000 cubic feet) we may better appreciate it if we remember that a French *savant* has computed that the stones of which it is composed would be sufficient to make a wall four feet high and one foot thick round the whole of France. In short, the Pyramid contains more stone than any single building ancient or modern. Those who have visited Luxor may be reminded that the Pyramid of Cheops covers a wider area than the Great Temple of Karnak.

The stupendous size of these monuments, and the incalculable amount of labour their building entailed, is not, however, so extraordinary as the astonishing architectural skill shown in the construction. As Fergusson observes, in his *History of Architecture*, notwithstanding the immense superincumbent weight, no settlement in any part can be detected to an appreciable fraction of an inch. In short, what probably first strikes the spectator is its matter, and then its manner of construction.

Ascent.—The ascent of the Great Pyramid, as usually undertaken, is not only absolutely free from danger but requires no climbing abilities at all. The only objection is, that it is rather trying to the wind and temper owing to the heat of the sun. Two or three Arabs practically haul the visitor up to the top, and, unless the tourist is strong-minded enough to take the initiative, only a couple of halts are, as a rule, allowed the breathless climber, and at these resting-places he will be pestered with unattached Arabs offering him water and clamouring for baksheesh.

The legal tariff is 2s. a head, which is paid to the Sheik of the Pyramids, but an additional sum, which varies according to the strength of mind (not of limb) and bargaining abilities of the traveller, has to be paid to the two Arabs told off to assist the climber. In the case of ladies and elderly persons a third claimant for baksheesh has to be reckoned with.

The summit reached, a magnificent view may be enjoyed during the regulation half-hour's rest. The Delta of the Nile, interspersed with countless channels and rivulets winding about like silver threads, seems to resemble the silver filigree ornaments of Genoa. Looking down at Cairo, from which the silver threads radiate, one is reminded of the fanciful Oriental comparison of the Delta to "a fan fastened with a diamond stud." The spectator's poetical fancies, however, are apt to be put incontinently to flight by clamorous demands for bakheesh on the part of the Arabs.

While resting on the summit, the Arab version of the Cumberland guides' race may be witnessed, as any of the Arab guides for a few piastres (at first the Arab will magnanimously offer to do the feat for five shillings) is quite willing to race up and down the Great and Second Pyramids in ten minutes.

The descent requires care, and even an experienced climber should not disdain the services of the Arabs, for a false step or slip might easily be fatal.

The feat of climbing the Second Pyramid (Chephren) had better not be emulated by the ordinary tourist, as the smooth granite casing still remains for some hundred and fifty feet from the top. To a mountaineer or cragsman, however, the climb is child's play, but even an experienced climber had better not attempt it in ordinary boots. Furnished with ordinary tennis shoes there would be little difficulty. Mark Twain, for instance, thought little of the feat.

Visit to Interior of Pyramids.—After the ascent, the exploration of the interior will probably be undertaken. This trip, though far more tiring than the climb to the summit, is particularly interesting and should not be omitted. Ladies, however, unless accustomed to scrambling, are not recommended to visit the interior. As in all the pyramids, the entrance is on the northern side. After descending a gallery some sixty feet, the passage which leads to the Great Gallery is reached. The inclined passage continues to a subterranean (or rather sub-pyramidal, for of course all the galleries and chambers in the interior are in a sense subterranean) chamber, known as the Queen's Chamber, which is rarely visited by ordinary tourists. The Great Gallery, still mounting upwards, leads to the King's Chamber, a room some 74 feet long, 17 broad, and 19 high. Here is the famous sarcophagus—the *raison d'être* indeed of the Great Pyramid—in which the remains of King Cheops no doubt once rested. The discovery of this red granite coffin did not, it is needless to say, upset the preconceived fantastic theories of Piazzi Smyth. Though obviously a sarcophagus, the professor declared that it was a coffer intended as an indestructible measure of capacity to all time!

The Sphinx.—The Sphinx, for thousands of years the greatest enigma in Egypt, has not succeeded in baffling the investigations of modern antiquarians, who have stripped it of much of the mystery, which constituted its great charm. Its builder, however, is still a matter of conjecture with students of Egyptology. It is now conclusively proved that it is nothing but a colossal image of the Egyptian deity, Harmachis, the "God of the Morning"; and therefore of his human representative, the king (unknown) who had it hewn. A stela found by Mariette near the Great Pyramid shows that the Sphinx was probably repaired by Cheops and Chephren, the builders of the Great and Second Pyramids respectively, which conclusively proves that it is older than either of these monuments.

The Sphinx is not an independent structure like the Pyramids, but is, for the most part, hewn out of the rocky cliff or promontory which juts out here from the desert plateau. The body and head are actually hewn out of this living rock, but sandstone masonry has been built up to correct the natural outline. The measurements given in many of the books of reference are of little value, as they vary according to the amount of sand which had drifted round the statue, but the latest measurements of Professor Petrie make the body 140 feet in length, while the head is about 30 feet from the forehead to the chin and 14 feet across. The front paws are

50 feet in length. The height of the figure is nearly 70 feet.

Some successful excavations at the foot of the Sphinx have recently been undertaken by an American Egyptologist, Colonel Raum. In 1896 he discovered the klaft or stone cap with the sacred asp on the forehead, which was known to have once been the head covering of the Sphinx. Dean Stanley, for instance, in his *Sinai and Palestine*, wonders, *apropos* of the colossal head, "what the sight must have been when on its head there was the royal helmet of Egypt."

A thorough and systematic excavation of this colossal figure, and the removal of the steadily encroaching desert sands which have buried the greater portion of the body is much to be desired. The cost, however, would be enormous, amounting at least to that of a whole year's excavation carried out by the joint efforts of the authorities of the National Museum and the Egypt Exploration Fund. Such a work should be undertaken by private enterprise. If another public-spirited man like Sir Erasmus Wilson would provide the funds for the work, it is believed that discoveries of the greatest importance would repay the work of excavating. The late Miss A. B. Edwards, indeed, was of opinion that the greatest find in the whole field of Egyptian antiquities would probably be round the base of the Sphinx, "which probably marks the site of a necropolis, buried a hundred feet in the sand, of the kings of the first and second dynasties!"

The first view of the Sphinx is undoubtedly striking and impressive in the highest degree, but it must be admitted that the conventional rhapsodies of modern writers who enlarge on the beauty of its features are over-strained. Before the figure had been mutilated by Mussulman fanatics it is possible that the mediæval critics were justified in speaking of the Sphinx as a model of human symmetry, wearing "an expression of the softest beauty and the most winning grace." Now, however, the traveller is confronted by a much-disfigured stone giant with a painfully distorted mouth, broken nostrils, and the grimace of a hideous negro. But though there is little concrete beauty in this colossal figure, there is an undeniable fascination about the Sphinx, due to its solemn surroundings, its mysterious traditions, and its immemorial antiquity.

To realise the charm of this monument we must read the classic and oft-quoted description of Kinglake, who, in a passage of incomparable prose, has succeeded where so many writers have failed.

"And near the Pyramids, more wondrous and more awful than all else in the land of Egypt, there sits the lonely Sphinx. Comely the creature is, but the comeliness is not of this world: the once worshipped beast is a deformity and a monster to this generation; and yet you can see that those lips, so thick and heavy, were fashioned according to some ancient mould of beauty—some mould of beauty now forgotten—forgotten because that Greece drew forth Cytherea from the flashing foam of the Ægean, and in her image created new forms of beauty, and made it a law among men that the short and proudly-wreathed lips should stand for the sign and the main condition of loveliness through all generations to come. Yet still there lives on the race of those who were beautiful in the fashion of the elder world; and Christian girls of Coptic blood will look on you with the sad serious gaze, and kiss you your charitable hand with the big pouting lips of the very Sphinx."

Campbell's Tomb is the best known of the royal sepulchres of this great cemetery of ancient Egyptian sovereigns. It is so called, in accordance with the popular and illogical method of nomenclature which formerly obtained of naming tombs after the discoverer or modern notability instead of the tenant, after the British Consul-general at the time of the discovery of the tomb by Colonel Howard Vyse. It is comparatively modern, being attributed by scholars to the twenty-sixth dynasty, when the dynasty of Sais with the help of Greek mercenaries over-ran Egypt. The tomb is really a pit about fifty-five feet deep. At the bottom is a small chamber in which were found four sarcophagi, one of which was given to the British Museum. It is a usual feat of the Arab guides to climb down the almost perpendicular sides of the shaft, but if strangers wish to explore the tomb chamber they will have to be let down by a rope—a feat which, considering the little there is to see at the bottom, is rarely performed. Of course there are numerous other tombs in the extensive necropolis which surrounds the Pyramids, but they are not of popular interest. The sight-seeing of most visitors to the pyramid field will, in short, be confined to the ascent of the Great Pyramid, possibly a visit to the interior, a hasty glimpse of the Sphinx, Campbell's Tomb, and the Sphinx Temple.

Temple of the Sphinx.—A short distance south of the Sphinx is the Temple of the Sphinx, a structure probably of the fourth dynasty. The sand-drift has so covered it that the non-observant traveller would suppose the temple to be a subterranean building. The Temple is a worthy pendant of the mighty mausoleum to which it seems to serve as a kind of mortuary chapel, for the discovery here of the famous green basalt statue of Khafra (Chephren) which we have seen in the Ghizeh Museum, is held by most authorities to prove that this sovereign was the builder of this temple as well as of the Second Pyramid. The temple is a fine specimen of the architecture of the Ancient Empire. It is lined in some parts with huge blocks of alabaster.

The above constitute the more popular sights in the Ghizeh Pyramid Field. There are, of course, many other ruins of tombs and temples scattered about this extensive plateau, but some archæological training and antiquarian study would be necessary for a proper appreciation of these remains.

II.—MEMPHIS AND SAKKARAH

Route.—The quickest and cheapest way of undertaking the excursion to these remarkable ruins is by rail. The nearest station, Bedrasheen, one hour and a half's ride by donkey from Sakkarah, is only 20 miles south of Cairo. There are two morning trains, a slow one leaving Cairo at 7 A.M. and reaching Bedrasheen in about an hour, and an express leaving at 8 A.M. which does the journey in three-quarters of an hour. For the return there is only one train viz. the mail train from Upper Egypt—for there are no local trains—which arrives at 5.28 P.M., reaching Cairo at 6.15 P.M. First-class fare, 23 piastres return. A pleasanter route is by the Nile. Messrs. Cook run a steam-launch every Wednesday for this excursion. The charge is 15s. per head, which includes donkey and fees to guides. Messrs. Gaze also organize excursions at frequent intervals. Lunch should be taken, though slight refreshments can be obtained at Bedrasheen Station.

History.—Memphis is said by some historians to have been founded by Menes, the first king of Egypt. At all events this ancient capital is of a very remote antiquity, and may probably rank with Heliopolis, Tanis, and other buried cities of the Delta as one of the oldest cities in the world.

But to whatever date we assign the foundation of Memphis—and all dates in the earliest periods of Egyptian history are merely approximate—there is no doubt that under the kings of the sixth dynasty Memphis was a great and splendid city. In the eighteenth dynasty Memphis, though still an important city and probably the capital of the Delta, had to resign to Thebes the position of metropolis of Egypt. After the New Empire Memphis declined, and its history for centuries is that of conquest in turn by Assyrian, Æthiopian, Persian, and Greek invaders. The building of Alexandria was the final blow to this decaying city, and the terrible prophecy of Jeremiah, "Memphis shall become a desert; she shall be forsaken and become uninhabited," was literally fulfilled.

Those who have visited Luxor and Karnak with their magnificent temples and monuments are perhaps puzzled to account for the total absence of any ruins of a city, which, though a couple of thousand years older than the City of a Hundred Gates, possessed many temples of later date than many of the splendid ruins of Thebes. The political and geographical conditions are, however, very different. Memphis lay in the path of all the invading nations who conquered Egypt in turn. Then Thebes had no Fostat or Cairo at its gates—a city for which the ruins of Memphis and Heliopolis served as building material. Then again the destructive character of the Nile floods to which low-lying Memphis was peculiarly subject, must not be forgotten. As Miss M. Brodrick in Murray's *Handbook for Egypt* well observes, "the waters of the inundation, long ago unrestrained by the protecting dykes, covered the plain with a gradually increasing layer of mud deposit, beneath which every trace of such ruins as were left completely disappeared."

The only antiquities at Memphis—for the tombs, pyramids, Apis Mausoleum are distinct and form part of the Memphian cemetery at Sakkarah—are the two colossal statues of Rameses II. The largest was presented to the English Government by Mehemet Ali, but no steps have ever been taken for its removal. It has been partially raised by a detachment of Royal Engineers under Major Bagnold, and is now concealed under a lofty wooden shed. Fee, 4 piastres, but those provided with the Government ticket for the Monuments (price £1 : 0 : 6) are admitted free. Both these statues are about 40 feet long, and are, no doubt, the twin colossi mentioned by Herodotus as having been erected by Sesostris (Rameses II.) in front of the Temple of Ptah.

Sakkarah is not more than a couple of miles from the statue of Rameses II. (the usual halting-place), but as the direct path is under water during the winter, travellers have to take a circuitous route some 5 or 6 miles long. The sights at Sakkarah are tombs and pyramids, the principal being the Mausoleum of the Sacred Bulls, usually called the Serapeum, the Step Pyramid, the Pyramid of Oonas, and the Tombs of Thi, Ptah-Hetep, and Mera. As this excursion entails rather hard work on the conscientious sightseer, ladies are recommended to ride the donkeys, (which are usually left at Mariette's House) to and from the different sites.

Serapeum.—This is certainly the most interesting of all the ancient monuments at Sakkarah. The sacred bulls were buried here from the eighteenth dynasty to the time of the Ptolemies, but only the portion of the mausoleum which formed the burial-place of these animals from 650 to 50 B.C. is now shown to visitors. Twenty-four of these mortuary chambers, each containing a sarcophagus averaging 13 feet long, 7 feet broad, and 11 feet high are to be seen. Only three of the later sarcophagi have any inscription. A ladder has been placed inside one of these colossal stone coffins to enable curious visitors to examine the interior. The fact that the Prince of Wales and his suite once took lunch in this bizarre dining-room will probably interest the average visitor more than any other item of information doled out by the ignorant guides!

This unique mausoleum was discovered by Mariette in 1860. He rightly conjectured that certain sphinxes met with in his excavations in various parts of Egypt, upon which were inscribed dedications to Osiris-Apis (whence the Greek Serapis), must refer to that long-lost Temple of Serapis near Memphis alluded to by Strabo. He was fortunate in his preliminary excavations, and soon lit upon the actual mausoleum.

The weight of these sarcophagi (some of which are estimated to weigh sixty-five tons), which all the efforts of Mariette's engineers to remove for transport to Ghizeh were absolutely ineffectual, is a striking testimony to the wonderful skill and resources of the ancient Egyptians, to whom such a task would have been child's play in comparison to the undertaking of removing the obelisks from Assouan to Lower Egypt. No remains of the sacred animals were found in any of the sarcophagi, all of which had evidently been rifled, probably at the time of the Arabian conquest of Egypt.

The history of the animal worship of the ancient Egyptians offers innumerable subjects of interest to the theologian as well as to the anthropologist and historian.

One of the most characteristic features of the ancient Egyptian faith was the reverence paid to certain animals. In some places the people worshipped the crocodile, in others the cat, in others, again, certain mythical birds and beasts; but especially it was the bull that was adored. At Heliopolis this animal was called Mnevis. At Memphis it was as Apis that he was reverenced. According to common belief, either the lightning or a moonbeam fecundated a cow, and the divinity then appeared upon earth in the shape of a bull. Special distinguishing marks guided the search for the sacred bull among the local herds. It sometimes happened that for years the priests were unable to discover the animal who, by certain complex external marks, corresponded to the ideal Apis.

A dramatic element is given to the discovery of the sepulchral chambers of the bulls. When Mariette effected an entrance he found on the layer of sand that covered the floor the *actual footprints of the workmen* who, 3700 years before, had laid the sacred mummy in its tomb, and closed the door upon it, as they believed for ever.

The fee for visiting the Apis Mausoleum and the tombs of Thi and Mera (except for visitors who are provided with the Government ticket for the Upper Nile Monuments) is 10 piastres.

Step Pyramid.—Owing to most travellers visiting Sakkarah and Memphis after Ghizeh the pyramids here usually only come in for very perfunctory notice. Yet the one known as the Step Pyramid—platform pyramid would perhaps convey a more accurate idea—is one of the most remarkable ancient monuments in Egypt.

If Mariette is correct in attributing it to Uenephes, a king of the first dynasty, either this or the False Pyramid of Medûm must be the *oldest historic building in the world.* It must have been in existence over two thousand years before Abraham was born.

Pyramid of Unas.—A small pyramid next the step pyramid, known as the Pyramid of Unas, is worth visiting. It has been opened up at the expense of Messrs. Thomas Cook and Sons, the well-known tourist agents. This was the sepulchre of the monarch whose remains are to be seen in the Ghizeh Museum, labelled with grim humour, "Fragments of King Unas"!

Among the tombs of the New Empire, the conventional term given by modern historians to denote the golden age of the eighteenth to the twenty-fifth dynasties, close to the Step Pyramid was found the famous stela known as the Tablet of Sakkarah. This, with the Abydos Tablet and the Turin Papyrus, are the chief authentic sources from which we derive our knowledge of the earliest period of Egyptian history. This tablet is now in the Ashmolean Museum at Oxford.

Tomb of Thi.—Thi was a priest of the fifth dynasty. His tomb or mastaba is close to Mariette's House, and is usually visited after the Serapeum. The tomb is one of the most interesting as well as the most elaborately decorated Ancient Empire tombs yet discovered, and deserves more attention than the ordinary tourist, who attempts to do Sakkarah in one day, can afford to devote to it. The chambers and corridors of the building, which is rather a subterranean temple than a tomb, are covered with paintings and sculpture most skilfully executed. The colours are remarkably vivid, and their preservation for so many thousands of years—for the Pompeii frescoes are but of yesterday in comparison—seems almost miraculous.

Tomb of Ptah-Hetep.—The Government grant, supplemented by fees from visitors, is insufficient for the effectual clearing of this and several other tombs, and it cannot now be seen by visitors. With the permission of the Director of the Ghizeh Museum the entrance, now choked with sand, can, it is true, be cleared away, but this would probably be at the expense of the visitor.

Tomb of Mera.—Since 1894 this tomb, which is almost as interesting as the two former, can be seen by visitors. It was only discovered in 1893 by M. de Morgan. It contains thirty-two chambers, which are elaborately decorated with paintings.

One of these paintings throws fresh light on the disputed question of the origin of chess. It represents Mera playing chess. Mera was an official of high rank under King Teta (whose pyramid is close to the tomb). This king belonged to the sixth dynasty, and his reign was assigned by Professor Lepsius to about the year 2700 B.C. Professor Brugsch, correcting this chronology, puts it back to a period still more remote, namely, to the year 3300 B.C., so that chess would appear to have been known in the once mysterious land of Mizraim something like 5200 years ago.

Pyramids of Dahshur.—These are about four miles from Sakkarah. They are seldom included in the day's excursion to Sakkarah, but there is no reason why an energetic tourist should not combine both. This is practicable by leaving Cairo by the 7 A.M. train for Bedrasheen, and hiring a donkey here. The boy should be told the day's programme or there may be difficulties later on. The chief places of interest at Sakkarah could be visited before lunch. In the afternoon ride to Dahshur and visit the Stone Pyramid, the Brick Pyramid, and the two discovered in 1896 by M. de Morgan (for permission to visit the two latter it is necessary to write in advance to the Director of the Ghizeh Museum). For the return journey take the 6.35 P.M. train from Assiout at Massounah Station (about 3 m. distant.) This station is nearer Dahshur than Bedrasheen Station, but the Upper Egypt mail train (arriving at Bedrasheen at 5.28 P.M.) does not stop here.

It is true that Dahshur is far more interesting to those fond of archæological studies than ordinary tourists. M. de Morgan has been very actively engaged in carrying on excavations here during the last few years. Among his principal discoveries were the beautiful jewellery of Princess Hathor in 1893, and, in the following year, the mummies of the two princesses of the twelfth dynasty, now to be seen in the Ghizeh Museum.

Sakkarah and the Pyramids in One Day.—Active tourists, accustomed to riding, might combine the Sakkarah trip with that to the Pyramids of Ghizeh by taking the 7. A.M. train to Bedrasheen, making a hurried visit to the Serapeum and principal tombs in the morning, and then after lunch riding along the desert plateau to the Pyramids (12 miles) returning thence to Cairo in the evening. It is, of course, a very tiring trip, but quite feasible for athletic visitors, and may be recommended to those who can only devote a week to Cairo.

No doubt the most satisfactory way of visiting the great Pyramid Field—for the Pyramids of Ghizeh, Sakkarah, and Dahshur are simply the principal mausolea of that vast necropolis which borders the Libyan Desert with "a fringe of gigantic cairns," for a distance of twenty miles—is to devote three or four consecutive days to their exploration, and camp out. Any Cairo dragoman would arrange this and would provide everything (tents, food, transport, etc.) for a party of not less than three at about £2 or £2 : 10s. per day per head, and relatively less for a week's excursion.

III.—HELIOPOLIS

The work of the sight-seer at Heliopolis is easy. There is only one curiosity, the famous obelisk, the sole relic of the ancient capital, which once ranked only second to Memphis in importance. This monument being the sole object of attraction for tourists, is naturally less perfunctorily examined than is the case at most other goals of travel in Egypt, where there is usually an embarrassing wealth of antiquities of all kinds. It is the oldest obelisk in Egypt yet remaining erect and *in situ*. The material is the usual rose-coloured granite of Assouan, the cradle of nearly all the Egyptian obelisks. Owing to a considerable part being buried in the soil and its somewhat commonplace surroundings, it lacks the dignity and impressiveness of the Theban obelisks. It is covered with hieroglyphics, which, as is the case with all well-known monuments in Egypt, have been carefully deciphered by Egyptologists, though they are now almost illegible, owing to bees having utilised the deeply incised hieroglyphics for their cells.

The only remains of the splendid Temple of Heliopolis built by Usertsen I. (twelfth dynasty) except the celebrated obelisk, are a few traces of brick wall. It was in front of this Temple of the Sun that the London Obelisk, "Cleopatra's Needle," stood for so many thousand years. The date of the city's foundation is even for Egypt of extreme antiquity. It is known that a king of the second dynasty established the cult of the Sacred Bulls both at On (Heliopolis) and Memphis, under the names of Mnevis and Apis respectively.

The sun is the most ancient object of Egyptian worship found upon the monuments. His birth each day when he springs from the bosom of the nocturnal heavens is the natural emblem of the eternal generation of the divinity. The rays of the sun, as they awakened all nature, seemed to give life to animated beings. Hence that which doubtless was originally a symbol became the foundation of the religion. It is the Sun (Ra) himself whom we find habitually invoked as the Supreme Being.

Heliopolis may be considered the mother-city of Baalbec, as, according to some historians, the Syrian "City of the Sun" was founded by a colony of priests who migrated from Heliopolis. The magnificent ruins of this Syrian Heliopolis, whose outer walls were composed of huge blocks, hardly excelled in size by those used for building the temples of Rameses the Great, will give some indication of the architectural splendour of the parent city which was not likely to be exceeded in splendour by the daughter settlement. According to recent measurements the largest of these blocks is sixty-four feet long, fourteen feet wide, and fourteen feet thick.

Matarieh is only a little more than a mile from Heliopolis, and those going by road will pass it on their way to the City of the Sun. According to the etymology of the village (place belonging to the Sun) it must originally have been an outlying portion of Heliopolis, and the famous Well was in fact the "Fountain of the Sun." The excursion from Cairo is particularly pleasant. Matarieh is charmingly situated, and from the number of palaces belonging to various members of the Khedivial family in its environs, might well be termed a village of palaces.

The chief interest to visitors lies in the famous Virgin's Tree and Virgin's Well. Under this holy tree the Virgin and Child are said to have rested after their flight into Egypt. The tree is a magnificent old sycamore, not, however, the kind of sycamore with which we are familiar and which belongs to the maple family, but a kind of fig. It need scarcely be said that the tree now seen is not the veritable tree of the legend, in fact even the guides do not dare to assert this. The tree is probably not more than three hundred years old. There is, however, little doubt but that it is planted on the site of an older tree to which the same tradition attaches. Many curious Coptic legends cluster round this venerable tree. According to some chroniclers the Virgin Mary hid herself from the soldiers of Herod among the branches, and there is a tradition that a spider by spinning a web effectually screened her hiding-place. These legends are a curious illustration of the proverbial repetition of history, or rather tradition, and recall to us the stories of Charles II. and the Boscobel Oak, and Robert Bruce and the spider.

The tree has been much hacked about by relic-hunting travellers, and the present proprietor, a Copt, with a sarcastic appreciation of the instincts of vandalism which seems to prompt latter-day tourists, has considerately planted another sycamore close by, from which pieces can be cut instead of from the original, a knife being chained to the tree for the purpose!

The late Khedive Ismail made a present of this tree to his guest, the Ex-Empress Eugenie, in 1869. The gift was graciously accepted, but the Empress's good taste prevented her taking any steps for the removal of this precious relic. Possibly too, she was aware of Ismail's practice of making presents of antiquities—obelisks, for instance—which were quite opposed to the wishes of the natives, or regarded the offer as an Oriental form of politeness never intended to be taken seriously, just as a modern Spanish grandee will not fail to tell a guest who incautiously admires any possession of his host, *Esta muy a la disposicion de Usted* (it is yours). This fictitious kind of hospitality is no doubt a traditionary habit bequeathed to Spaniards by their Saracenic conquerors.

The Virgin's Well is close by, and round this spot also have centred many early Christian legends. It has earned peculiar sanctity as the well in which the Holy Child was bathed. The fact that the water is fresh, being fed from springs, while that of most wells in the delta is either salt or brackish, naturally gives colour to this tradition. According to the Coptic legend the water was salt until the Virgin bathed her Child in it.

The balsam shrub, the balm of Gilead of the Bible, formerly grew here in profusion. The balsam plants are said to have been brought from Judæa to this spot by Cleopatra; who, trusting to the influence of Anthony, removed them, in spite of the opposition of Herod. The plants were in later times taken from

Matarieh to Arabia and grown near Mecca, whence the balsam is now brought to Egypt and Europe, under the name of Balsam of Mecca; and the gardens of Heliopolis no longer produce this valuable plant. A still more profitable article of commerce, namely cotton, one of the most lucrative in Egypt, sprang from some experiments in the culture of this plant at Matarieh in 1820.

A visit to an ostrich farm in the village is usually included in the day's excursion, but unless the visitor has plenty of time at his disposal, he should resist the importunities of the guide and forgo this excursion. An ostrich farm, whether in Algeria, the Cape, New Zealand, or Egypt, does not offer much variety.

The attendant expects a fee of 4 piastres. The excursion to Heliopolis and Matarieh can be easily managed in an afternoon as there is a railway station at Matarieh (fare from Cairo, 1st ret., 4½ piastres), where donkeys can be hired for the Virgin's Tree and Heliopolis for a few piastres. The tariff for a cab from Cairo allowing two hours' wait is 40 piastres, but if Matarieh is to be included the driver will expect a few piastres extra.

IV.—HELOUAN-LES-BAINS

Helouan-les-Bains, which is about sixteen miles from Cairo, on the east side of the Nile, is situated on a desert plateau at the foot of the Tûra hills, and is about two miles from the Nile, to which a carriage road bordered with trees has lately been constructed. Helouan is quite modern, and is, in fact, a kind of artificial oasis in the desert. It was the favourite residence of the late Khedive Thewfik, and it was here that this amiable and enlightened sovereign died.

Though it makes an interesting minor desert excursion, its chief claim to notice is as a health resort.

Now that the concession from the Egyptian Government has been granted to an English company —the contract dating from 1896—a new era of prosperity for this rising winter station is practically assured. Under the previous concession to a German Syndicate, the management of the Bathing Establishment in connection with the Sulphur Springs was not carried out in conformity with European ideas, and the Baths of Helouan "hung fire." The new concession (45 years) to the Helouan and Cairo Railway Company is favourably commented upon by Lord Cromer in his last report (1897):—"The whole system, is, I understand to be remodelled and improved. The chief hotel, which has been re-constructed, as well as the baths themselves, have been placed under the charge of a resident English doctor (Dr. Page May). As the waters are said to be specially suited to the alleviation of certain complaints, it is not improbable that the town of Helouan will before long develop into a largely frequented winter resort."

Route.—The railway station for Helouan is at Bab-el-Luk close to the Place Abdin. The railway is not one of the Government lines, but the property of the Helouan Baths Company, and consequently the Zone system of fares adopted for places near Cairo is not in use. Trains are frequent, and the journey takes less than half-an-hour. An omnibus from the two hotels meets the trains.

Hotels.—There are two good hotels, Grand Hotel de Helouan and Grand Hotel des Bains. The former, facing the Casino Gardens and Railway Station, is a large, first-class house. It is fitted with electric light, and has large billiard, reading, and smoking rooms, also lawn-tennis courts. There is a post and telegraph office in the grounds. The hotel was built in 1891 according to the best European methods. It has recently been enlarged, two wings having been added. Tariff from twelve shillings a day. The Grand Hotel des Bains is close to the Bathing Establishment, and is intended mainly for invalids and others who come on account of the sulphur and iron baths. The terms are a little more moderate than at the other hotel, the daily pension being only ten shillings, but the furniture, appointments, and service are little inferior to those of the larger hotel. The sanitation of both has been carefully looked after by sanitary engineers, and approved by the Egyptian Public Health Department.

Villas and Apartments.—Unlike Cairo, where villas are notoriously scarce and dear, there are a large number of villas, both furnished and unfurnished, which can be rented at a moderate rent. In fact Helouan, with its excellent train services, resident English doctor and chaplain (Rev. W. Bateman Blake), is gradually becoming a kind of residential suburb of Cairo. Nearly all the villas are built in the Oriental style with flat roofs, which are, of course, better adapted for the desert climate than European buildings.

The Baths.—The directorate have some ground for their proud boast that they control the oldest health resort in the world, for many historians are of opinion that the springs are those said to be "at the quarries on the east side of the Nile," where according to the Ptolemian historian, Manetho, King Amenophis (Amen-hetep I., *circa* 1600 B.C.) sent the "leprous and other cureless persons, in order to separate them from the rest of the Egyptians."

To the invalid, however, it is of more importance to know that the new *Etablissement des Bains* is being re-constructed and put on a footing with any similar establishment in Europe.

"There are about a dozen thermal springs, which give water in abundance of three different kinds—viz., sulphur water, saline water, and mild chalybeate water. The water commonly used for drinking purposes and that used in the baths rises from the earth at a temperature of 86° to 90°, and at the rate of over forty gallons a minute. The water contains small quantities of iron, aluminia, and other salts. Its chief ingredients, according to analysis, are in the following proportions per gallon: sodium chloride, 355 grains; calcium carbonate, 58; magnesium sulphate, 36; sulphuretted hydrogen, 6½. The sulphur water is not only richer in sulphur constituents than the water which has made the fame of Aix-les-Bains, but is equal to the strongest sulphur waters of Harrogate; it also contains nearly three times as much salts as the well-known waters of Bath. The saline and chalybeate waters are of a similar composition to the above, and are very fair waters of their class. Strange to say, however, these waters are not much known. The reason for this is not difficult to see. Formerly the bathing establishment was quite out of keeping with European ideas." Fortunately the late concession from the Egyptian Government for the baths terminated last year (1896), and the new *concessionaires* have planned the baths with the approval of the Public Works Department. There being only nominal ground-rents to pay in the desert, space is no object; and the dressing-rooms, cooling-rooms, douche-rooms, etc., are very large, and well ventilated and lighted. Adjoining the baths establishment, is a gentleman's swimming bath, 70 yards long by 25 yards broad.

The new Baths "will probably be completed during the present winter" (1897-8).

Treatment.—The Baths are recommended by medical men for gout, rheumatism, sciatica, and certain skin diseases, as well as for persons suffering from gastric disorders. Then apart from the "cure" a winter at Helouan can be safely recommended to those in the early stages of pulmonary consumption and persons with delicate chests. The Bathing Establishment is under the control of an English medical man, Dr. Page May.

Amusements.—There is a small casino where occasional dances, concerts, and theatrical performances are given, and there are tennis courts in the grounds. Then some small golf links have been laid out, which will at any rate enable devotees of the "royal and ancient game" to keep up their practice in the winter. Once a week during the season a military band from Cairo plays in the Casino gardens.

Helouan makes a good centre for small desert trips, and excursions to the Tûra and Masara Quarries, the Petrified Forest, etc. Sakkarah and Memphis also can easily be reached by visitors, as a small tram-line to the Nile (about three miles distant) has recently been laid. It is true that there are no trams as yet, and visitors are propelled in a trolly by Arabs. Donkeys and sand-carts and even camels can be hired at the hotels, and there is also a small steam-launch on the Nile which can be hired for the day or week by visitors. Sportsmen will find a certain amount of game in the neighbourhood, but the "hyænas, gazelles, and antelopes" and other big game, which are alluded to in certain printed descriptions of Helouan are, of course, to say the least, so scarce as to be practically non-existent within a reasonable distance (See "Sporting Trips").

Excursions.—The most interesting excursion is the one to the ancient Pharaonic quarries of Tûra, which are still worked. These quarries can boast of an even earlier history than that of the period which is somewhat loosely termed Pharaonic (an epithet which strictly refers to the sovereigns of the eighteenth, nineteenth, and twentieth dynasties), as most Egyptologists are agreed that the casing-stones of some of the Pyramids were quarried at Tûra. Fortunately the quarrying at the present day is, for the most part, confined to the surface rock, so that visitors can see the very caverns excavated by the Pharaohs almost as they were when the ancient quarrymen laboured there. In one of these caverns are sculpture reliefs representing Amen-em-hat, (eighteenth dynasty) sacrificing to the gods Amen and Horus. Tablets of other sovereigns of this dynasty have also been discovered.

Tûra is probably the Troja of Strabo and Diodorus. These historians, probably misled by the similarity of the ancient name (Ta-ro-fu) did not hesitate to call it Troja, and as a plausible pretext declared that it was so called because the captive Trojans, who were said by Herodotus to have followed King Menelaus to Egypt, had a settlement here. It is curious how many myths, gravely set down as authentic history by Diodorus, Strabo, Herodotus and other great writers, are due to errors in etymology.

These quarries are probably the oldest in the world, older even than those of Assouan. Many of these are still in use, and it is curious to think that the streets of the modern city of Cairo are paved with flags of the same magnesium limestone that the Egyptian masons used for building the temples of Memphis over four thousand years ago.

The best way of reaching these ancient quarries is to take the train to the next station, Masara, and then walk to the quarries, the nearest of which is some two or three miles off; or donkeys could be hired at the hotel, and the railway could be dispensed with. The ride through the desert plateau is very interesting. If this method be chosen the whole morning must be devoted to this excursion.

Another interesting desert trip is to the plain of petrified wood, grandiloquently called by the guides the Petrified Forest. This is more easily reached from Helouan than Cairo, the usual starting-place (For description see "Minor Excursions").

V.—MINOR EXCURSIONS

It is not altogether surprising that the list of minor excursions recommended in the standard guide-books, and known to the local guides and dragomans should be such a meagre one. The ancient monuments of Ghizeh, Memphis, Heliopolis, etc., to say nothing of the important examples of Saracenic architecture with which Cairo abounds, are so numerous and engrossing that tourists, making only a short stay in the Egyptian capital, cannot spare the time for ordinary drives and excursions. Those, however, who are making Cairo their headquarters for the winter, would find innumerable objects of interest to occupy their energies after exhausting the regulation sights.

The Petrified Forest.—This is an expedition which should not be omitted by strangers, for though there is little to see at the Forest itself but a few fossilised trunks, the ride on donkey-back makes a pleasant little desert trip, and the route across a spur of the Mokattam Mountains affords magnificent views of Cairo, much better than those obtained from the Citadel, and at sunset the atmospheric effects of the desert are superb. It is possible to drive, for the rough track which is dignified by the name of road is practicable for wheeled vehicles, but this mode of locomotion will not be found at all satisfactory, and it is far preferable, even for ladies, to make the trip in the orthodox way on donkeys. A guide is quite unnecessary as every donkey-boy knows the way.

The journey there and back can be comfortably managed in a single morning, if an early start be made, though the guides will naturally insist that it is a whole day's excursion. No doubt, for the Great Petrified Forest a whole day should be allowed, but the ride is tedious and a little too tiring for all but the most robust. If ladies attempt it they should at all events be careful to see that their mount has a well-fitting saddle. A halt is usually made at the so-called Moses' Well. It need scarcely be said that there is not even the slightest legendary association with Moses, but the Arabs are fond of naming geographical features after famous Biblical characters. This spring is in a gorge of one of the Mokattam Mountains, and the small Petrified Forest could be reached by active pedestrians by climbing the crest of the Mountain. The mounted members of the party must, however, return to the mouth of the ravine and follow the path that winds round the spur of the hill, when the forest will be reached in about half an hour. The remains of the fossil trees strew the plateau for several miles. It remains a moot point with geologists whether the trees are indigenous, or whether they were floated by water and became embedded in the ground, being converted in the course of many thousands of years into stone.

The distance from the citadel is between five and six miles only, but four hours should be allowed for the excursion. There is no regular tariff for donkeys, and a bargain should be struck beforehand. Eight or ten piastres would be liberal.

The Great Petrified Forest is some eight miles further, and the excursion, which takes the whole day, is an extremely fatiguing one, and seldom attempted by the average tourist. For one thing few of the Cairo donkey-boys know the way. The precise directions given in Baedeker should, however, suffice to those who know how to use a map. For this excursion a horse is preferable to a donkey.

The Barrage.—The Barrage is a huge dam or weir built across the Nile at the head of the Delta, at the point where the Rosetta and Damietta branches of the Nile unite. The Barrage is consequently a double one, and each is connected by a high wall nearly two miles in length. This wall serves as a kind of rampart, for the Barrage was originally planned as a fort and barracks as well as a dam. The eastern portion of the Barrage which spans the Damietta branch—here a noble river wider than the Thames at Gravesend—is some 600 yards long, while the portion which crosses the Rosetta branch is a little over 500 yards long. There are some hundred and thirty arches altogether, the span of each being sixteen feet.

The Barrage, which is 15 miles by train from Cairo, is now easily reached as a branch line, connecting with the main line from Cairo to Alexandria, has recently been laid. There are half a dozen trains daily each way. First-class fare, 6 piastres return. The excursion can easily be managed between breakfast and lunch, a convenient train leaving Cairo at 8.30 A.M., while a train leaves the Barrage at 12.15. The journey takes a little under an hour.

The object of this colossal dam is to serve as a reservoir during low Nile. In theory the conception was a grand one, and full credit should be given to Mehemet Ali who first saw the possibility of bringing an enormous area of the delta under cultivation, which hitherto, for want of any means of irrigation, was absolutely unproductive. Unfortunately, the original engineers seem to have bungled and did not make the foundations strong enough, so that, from its completion in 1867 till 1885, when Sir Colin Scott Moncrieff, the head of the Public Works Department, undertook the task of restoring it, it was looked upon as a kind of white elephant by the Egyptian Government.

The history of the Barrage is interesting. It was a project like the Suez Canal, which doubtless Napoleon would have carried out had his scheme of conquering Egypt succeeded. Then Mehemet Ali began it, and it was abandoned by Said Pasha. Abbas Pasha spent considerable sums in futile tinkering of the work. In 1885 Sir Colin Moncrieff and his staff of engineers made an exhaustive examination of the structure. He found that the arches of the Damietta branch were badly cracked and that the whole structure was faultily built, and though an English board of engineers had declared that to rebuild the Barrage and make it of any practicable use £1,200,000 would be required, Sir Colin, after six years' continuous labour, succeeded in making the two dams thoroughly serviceable at an expenditure of little more than a third of the estimate of the English experts.

The Barrage as it now stands—remodelled, restored, and thoroughly serviceable—is an excellent illustration of the splendid work carried out within recent years in the irrigation of Egypt. All efforts to ameliorate the condition of life among the fellaheen are summed up in a thorough system of irrigation. In Egypt, indeed, so far as practical benefit to the community is concerned, irrigation and drainage are of equal importance with improvements in means of locomotion in other countries—railways, bridges, roads, and other remunerative public works.

The expedition would be rendered less fatiguing by returning by the western bank of the Nile, as this would save the long walk or ride over both branches of the Barrage and back to the Barrage Station. The itinerary would be as follows. Train from Cairo to the Barrage Station, then walk across the Damietta and Rosetta Barrages to Manashee Station, which is close to the western end of the Rosetta Barrage. Though there are very few trains on this branch railway there is a convenient one leaving Manashee at 12.53, arriving at Cairo at 1.50. If lunch be taken along with the visitor, he could get out at Bachatil Station, and visit the site of the Battle of the Pyramids.

Shubra.—It is a very pretty drive along the famous Shubra Avenue (once the fashionable promenade of Cairo) to Shubra Palace. The Palace is not worth visiting, but the gardens are charming.

VI.—SPORTING TRIPS

THE sportsman is naturally inclined to question the existence of good shooting or fishing within a reasonable distance of a fashionable winter resort like Cairo. However, very tolerable snipe and quail shooting in their respective seasons can be obtained even within an hour's ride of the Egyptian capital. In fact, during the winter months a fair bag of snipe may be made almost at the threshold of the city in the cultivated ground between the Pyramids and the Nile. This district, however, is more noted for its quail shooting. Indeed, if we compare the sporting capabilities of the various winter stations on the shores of the Mediterranean, we shall find that better shooting is to be had within a few hours of Cairo, than can be obtained in the neighbourhood of Ajaccio, Corfu, or Tangier, which are popularly supposed to be the best sporting centres among Mediterranean winter resorts. The best shooting in Egypt, with the exception of big game, is to be found in the Delta, and, speaking generally, the further one goes south the scarcer is the game—snipe for instance are rarely shot south of the Fayyoum, *pace* certain guide-books which speak of snipe being plentiful in the Theban plain near Luxor.

These venatorial limitations should be kept in mind by the sporting visitor, who might naturally suppose that by going further afield, and by leaving the densely populated Delta he would meet with more success. As a matter of fact, Egypt being essentially an agricultural country, density of population implies a great deal of cultivated ground, while in the sparsely-populated fringe of desert bordering the Upper Nile there is very little cultivation to afford the necessary cover for the birds.

Snipe and quail are the game *par excellence* of Egypt, and therefore a short description of the best shooting-grounds which can be conveniently reached from Cairo may prove of service.

The quail affords sport all over the Delta in the early spring months, when the birds come down the Nile Valley on their annual migration to their northern breeding-grounds. In size and appearance the quail is very like a small partridge, while their markings are like those of the snipe. When put up, their flight is quick and straight. They are slow to rise as a rule and are often walked over. They afford excellent sport, and if there is any wind they may easily be missed. They are usually found in clover, lupins, or wheat near water. The same locality usually serves for snipe in the winter months and quail in the spring.

Mena House Hotel (near the Pyramids) or the Barrage make a convenient centre for a day's shooting. The latter is reached by train in about an hour from Cairo (see "Minor Excursions"). The officials at the Barrage are courteous and willing to give advice to strangers as to the best places for snipe or quail. The Barrage is close to the new Barrage Station.

On the main line from Cairo to Alexandria is the flourishing town of Benha, about thirty miles from Cairo (reached in a little under an hour), and in the fields and plantations near this town game is fairly plentiful. Then this district has the advantage of not being so much shot over as the Barrage shooting-ground, which is much frequented by English officers stationed at Cairo. As a rule better sport is obtainable during a high Nile season than when the river is low.

An excellent shooting-ground for all kinds of wild-fowl, as well as snipe and quail, is the country between Zagazig (half-way between Cairo and

Ismailia, and easily reached by rail from Cairo) and Tel-el-Kebir, memorable for the defeat of Arabi's troops in 1882. Game is plentiful along the banks of the Fresh Water Canal, which runs parallel to the lines raised by the rebel general. This is a two days' expedition, but tolerable sleeping accommodation is to be had at the Zagazig Station. Zagazig, too, being an important town, provisions and most necessities for camping out can be obtained here.

For the more distant shooting excursions it is the best plan to camp out and make up one's mind to be independent of native inns—for the lack of suitable accommodation in the villages of the Delta is the one great drawback to sport in Egypt. It is advisable to leave all the arrangements to a dragoman or *shikari*, easily obtained at Cairo through the hotel manager or the tourist agencies, who would contract to supply a party of sportsmen with tent, food, bedding and other essentials for from 25s. to 30s. a day inclusive per head, for a period of not less than a week. The Egyptian climate is well adapted for tenting expeditions. Atfeh, some fifty miles up the Nile, the Fayyoum, Port Said, and Damietta will be found the best centres for more ambitious sportsmen. These places are the most accessible, but there are few places in the Delta where a fairly good bag of quail cannot be obtained in the early spring months.

Atfeh is not far from Wasta (a station on the Nile railway some sixty miles south of Cairo), but on the opposite bank of the Nile. The village lies almost directly opposite Medûm, which is familiar to tourists as the site of the famous False Pyramid, a ruin of even earlier date than the Pyramid of Cheops, in fact, according to some Egyptologists, it is the oldest ruin in Egypt.

But for a week's camping-out expedition, there can be no doubt that the Fayyoum affords better sport than any district in the Delta. Game of all kinds is exceedingly plentiful, and besides snipe and quail, good bags of partridge and sand-grouse (called by the Arabs *kata* from the peculiar cry of the bird) as well as duck can be obtained.

Camping-out is not absolutely necessary, as tolerable accommodation can be had at Medina (sometimes called Fayyoum) the capital of this richly cultivated region, and through the enterprise of the Government two light railways diverge from Medina to Sennoures and Abouxa, both well-known sporting rendezvous, and a railway unites Medina with Wasta.

The Lake Birket-el-Karoun, which, next to Lake Menzaleh, affords the best wild-fowl shooting in Egypt, is only about five miles from Abouxa.

For about 4s. or 5s. a day, a local *shikari* can be obtained at Wasta or Medina, who would act as porter and beater. An introduction, easily obtained from the Ministry of the Interior at Cairo, to the Mudir at Medina, will be a wise precaution, especially as the shooting and fishing is preserved in some parts of the Fayyoum. The snipe shooting on the banks of the Yusuf Canal is excellent, over fifty brace a day per gun being sometimes obtained in January and February—the best months.

Big game is very scarce in Lower Egypt, but wild boar are sometimes found on the shores of Lake Birket-el-Karoun; and even near Cairo, in the Gebel Mokattam range, and beyond the Ghizeh Pyramids, it is still possible to pot an occasional hyæna, wolf, or jackal. The assistance of local guides will be necessary, as casual lying in wait on a moonlight night at the supposed haunt of these animals is of little use, without the co-operation of the natives. The usual method is to bait a likely spot with the carcase of a donkey or some other domestic animal, which means a considerable outlay of baksheesh on the part of the tourist.

As to outfit, an ordinary shooting suit or a suit of washing *Khaki* would be found most serviceable, but for head-gear a helmet or terai hat should replace the ordinary cap. As the mud in the swamps and marshes will be found particularly heavy and tenacious when going after duck or snipe, the best foot-gear is a pair of shooting-boots (designed by Rev. C. G. Griffenhoofe), fitted with uppers of strong canvas reaching almost to the knee and fastened with a strap or buckle, but laced down the front. The opening should be closed as well with a wide tongue. These boots can be easily washed clean of mud, and in drying they never shrink.

A useful and well-informed chapter on shooting in the neighbourhood of Cairo, will be found in a little book called *Wintering in Egypt*, by Dr. A. J. M. Bentley and Rev. C. G. Griffenhoofe (see "Bibliography"). To this instructive little volume, I am indebted for some of the information given above.

Since '94 the import of loaded cartridges has been strictly prohibited by the Egyptian War Office, so tourists wishing to shoot are recommended to bring blank cartridges with them and get them loaded in Cairo, or the cartridges can be obtained at Baiocchi, the principal Cairo gunsmith, for about sixty-five or seventy piastres per 100. No. 8 shot is best for snipe or quail, and No. 4 for duck and teal.

Though no game licence is required in Egypt, yet a licence to carry fire-arms is officially required, and is occasionally asked for in the neighbourhood of Cairo. Then, though there is little private preserving, it must be remembered that in certain districts the shooting as well as the fishing is farmed out by the Government. Certain portions of Lake Menzaleh and Birket-el-Karoun are thus preserved, and strangers will have to obtain special permission to shoot or fish over these prohibited areas from the Mudir or local authorities. Sportsmen, too, should be careful about shooting pigeons in the near neighbourhood of a village, as they are often alleged to be domestic ones.

Though Egypt has deservedly acquired the reputation of being one of the most expensive winter residences for Europeans, yet few places within a week of London offer such excellent opportunities for fishing and shooting at so moderate an outlay, supposing, of course, the visitor is prepared to scorn the delights of a fashionable Cairo hotel. Provided he speaks a little Arabic,[1] and does not mind rough, but homely, accommodation in the inns of the Delta towns and villages, he can get as much shooting and fishing as he cares for at a total expenditure daily of not more than he would pay for board at a cheap Riviera *Pension*.

[1] A very serviceable list of sporting phrases is given in C. A. Thimm's *Modern Egyptian Phrase-book*. Price 2s. E. Marlborough and Co., London.

PART III

THE NILE AND ITS MONUMENTS

I.—THE NILE FROM CAIRO TO LUXOR

Routes.—The Nile voyage can be done in various ways, according to the length of the traveller's purse and the amount of time at his disposal.

1. **Dahabeah.**—This is the time-honoured mode of Nile travel, and is no doubt the ideal one, but except for a party of at least seven or eight it is a decidedly costly means of conveyance (see "The Nile as a Health Resort").

2. **Tourist Steamer.**—The itineraries of these steamers are planned in the special interest of sight-seers, and for travellers of a social and gregarious disposition there can be no more comfortable, and indeed luxurious, method of doing the temples and ruins of Upper Egypt. One of the fine saloon steamers of Messrs. Cook leaves Cairo every Tuesday at 10 A.M. For a twenty days' voyage to Luxor and Assouan and back the fare, which includes all expenses, board, conveyance to or from the temples, backsheesh, service of dragoman, medical attendance

(fee optional), etc., is £50; to Wady Halfa, £73. In the height of the season there is an extra trip to the First Cataract and back, occupying four weeks. Fare £65. During the season 1897-98 the steamer *Mohammed Ali* leaves Cairo for this trip on January 5th. This steamer is smaller than those in the regular service, taking from forty to fifty instead of seventy to eighty passengers. The famous triad of Rameses steamers are reserved for the regular service. These saloon steamers are perhaps the most luxurious and best appointed river steamers in the world. They are, however, apt to be very crowded—the most popular vessel, *Rameses the Great*, having had every berth taken during the last six seasons. This very popularity, indeed, constitutes the chief objection in the opinion of many travellers, and the smaller and less luxurious, but in many respects equally comfortable, steamers of the Thewfikieh line (Gaze and Sons, Ltd.) are preferred. The *Rameses the Great* and *Rameses III.* are new boats, 220 and 200 feet long respectively. They have steel hulls and powerful engines (500 horse-power) of the latest pattern. The state-rooms in no case contain more than two berths, and each steamer has a number of single-berthed cabins. The state-rooms are fitted with electric bells and the electric light, while the windows have a triple arrangement of sliding glass, venetian and wire gauze. There are bath-rooms fitted with hot and cold water and every modern arrangement. The dining saloons are upon the upper deck forward. Every steamer has a reading saloon and a library containing a number of interesting works on Egypt. Each steamer is supplied with refrigerating chambers and ice-making machines. The steamer is under the control of a competent European manager, and carries one or more dragomans, who act as guides and interpreters on shore. An English doctor accompanies each vessel, whose services are at the disposal of passengers without charge, though fees are almost invariably given. Though the fares may seem high in comparison with the time occupied and the mileage covered, yet it must be admitted that the catering and service in these floating hotels is equal to that of ocean liners.

The mail steamers of the Thewfikieh Company are comfortable and well-found boats, and are popular with many travellers owing to the comparatively small number of passengers and the extremely moderate fares. Their cheap service to Assouan and back (seventeen days), leaving Cairo every ten days, costs only £22. Then every week from January to March there is the regular trip to Luxor and Assouan and back. Time, 3 weeks. Fare, £35. This is the cheapest Nile voyage available, and actually costs less than a stay of the same period at a fashionable Cairo hotel. On December 20th takes place the first sailing of Gaze's new steamer *Columbia*, specially built for Nile traffic.

3. **Mail Steamer.** — The Government Mail Steamers are under the control of Messrs. Cook. On each there is accommodation for only thirty-two first-class passengers. They leave every Tuesday and Saturday at 9 A.M. from the 14th December. Special arrangements are made for tourists, and there is an inclusive fare of £25 for the return voyage from Cairo to Assouan (nineteen days) which includes board on steamer and a week's hotel accommodation divided between the Luxor and Assouan hotels. For those who cannot afford three weeks for the Nile, the trip can be shortened to eight days by taking the railway from Cairo to Nagh Hamadi (the present terminus of the Upper Nile railway) and back. Fare for this combined rail and steamer service is £21. This includes three days' hotel accommodation at Luxor.

These mail steamers do not, however, afford much opportunity for sight-seeing between Cairo and Luxor, owing to the exigencies of the public service.

4. **Rail and Steamer Combined.**—Travellers who can tolerate the poor accommodation of native inns, can visit the principal antiquities of the Upper Nile at little cost by travelling independently of the

tourist arrangements. The first-class railway fare from Cairo to Nagh Hamadi is only £1 : 15 : 9, while the first-class fare on the mail steamer from the latter to Luxor is only £1 : 5 : 9, and to Assouan £3 : 14 : 3. In fact the through fare (first-class) from Cairo to Wady Halfa is only £9 : 12 : 6, but this does not, of course, include meals, for which 10 frs. a day is charged. The journey between Cairo and Nagh Hamadi could be broken at Minieh or Roda (for Beni Hassan and Tel-el-Amarna) and Balliana (for Abydos), and passable sleeping accommodation is obtainable at these towns.

Nine out of ten travellers hurry on to the ruins of the Theban Plain, Philæ, or Abou Simbel, and leave the ancient temples and tombs which bestrew the Nile valley between Cairo and Luxor for a hurried and somewhat perfunctory inspection on the return voyage, when, sated with the architectural splendours of Ancient Thebes, the less striking monuments north of Luxor come as an anti-climax. Yet these remains are from an antiquarian point of view even more interesting than the Middle Empire ruins of Thebes, or the architectural trophies of the Ptolemies that stud the beautiful island of Philæ. We are all apt to forget, as Miss A. B. Edwards is careful to remind her readers, that the ancient history of Egypt goes against the stream. If we omit the conjectural, perhaps mythical, site of This, which is almost prehistoric, it is in the Delta and on the banks of the Lower Nile that relics of the most ancient cities are to be found, at Tanis, Memphis, and Heliopolis, for instance, while the latest temples and tombs are found in the Upper Nile valley and in Nubia.

The first hundred and fifty miles of the journey up the Nile is often complained of as being wearisome and monotonous, and between Memphis and Beni-Hassan, no doubt, the ruins are few and unimportant. Still this scenic monotony is perhaps subjective rather than objective. To one lacking in imagination, no doubt a great London highway like the Strand would be monotonous, while another would find the same fault with the Alps because each peak seems to him very like another.

Beni-Hassan, 170 miles from Cairo, is remarkable for the famous rock tombs excavated in terraces on the precipitous bank of the Nile. The cliff has been cut through by the river, which formerly reached to its foot, but has since retired, so that a considerable expanse of plain (an hour's ride) lies between the tombs and the Nile. These tombs belong to the twelfth dynasty, which dates from about 3000 to 2500 B.C. There are about fifteen, but only two of them, those of Ameni or Amen-Em-hat, and

Khnemn-hetep II. are likely to interest the average sight-seer.

To the artist these famous grottoes are of the highest interest as the birthplace of Greek decorative art. The principal sculptural ornaments, such as the spiral, the key pattern, and the so-called honeysuckle pattern—the latter, according to Professor Flinders Petrie, a florid imitation of the Egyptian lotus pattern—which are often regarded as purely Greek in origin, are undoubtedly Egyptian. "They were all painted on the ceilings of the Beni-Hassan tombs full twelve hundred years before a stone of the treasuries of Mycenæ or Orchomenos was cut from the quarry." The spiral is continually found, either in its simplest form or combined with the lotus, in the decorations of these tombs. The columns in the porches of these tombs are technically known as proto-doric, and, as the name implies, are prototypes of the well-known Doric columns.

An Egyptian origin may also be allowed to the Ionic column. The lotus leaf design, a characteristic decorative feature of this class of column, "furnished the architects of the Ancient Empire with a noble and simple model for decorative purposes. Very slightly conventionalised, it enriches the severe façades of tombs of the fourth, fifth, and sixth dynasties, which thus preserve for us one of the earliest motives of symmetrical design in the history of ornament."

The walls are covered with paintings which represent scenes in the life of the deceased, and form a kind of pictorial biography, which are not, as in the case of the paintings of later tombs, intermingled with the conventional mystic representations of divinities.

The Tomb of Khnemn-Hetep II. is in the northern group of tombs. The principal chamber or shrine contains a large figure of the deceased, who was one of the feudal lords of Egypt in the time of the twelfth dynasty. This tomb is usually known as No. 1, for all the tombs here are numbered. It is best known for the painting which is supposed, but on doubtful authority, to represent Joseph and his brethren arriving in Egypt to buy corn. At all events it represents the arrival in Egypt of a band of foreigners, thirty in number, who, from their features, seem to belong to the Semitic race.

Equally interesting is the TOMB OF AMENI, a high functionary of the court of Usertsen I. (twelfth dynasty). One painting in the picture gallery of this tomb describes pictorially his expedition into Ethiopia and his triumphant return, laden with spoil and trophies.

Speos Artemidos.—In addition to the Tombs

there is a kind of rock temple dedicated to the lion-headed goddess, Sechet or Pasht, called Artemis (Diana) by the Greeks, which is known as the Speos Artemidos (the cave of Artemis). It is excavated in a rock at the entrance of a gorge half an hour's ride from the Tombs. This temple was begun by Thothmes III. and the famous queen Hatshepsu, and was embellished with a few sculptures by Seti I., but was never completed. The only finished reliefs are on the inner wall of the portico, and as they are of a good period of Egyptian art, it is to be regretted that the other sculptures are in an unfinished state.

Between Beni Hassan and the Theban Plain, ruins of temples and tombs, Roman forts, eyrie-like convents, grottoes, etc., abound, and the Nile voyager is rarely out of sight of some ancient monument. To visit all would, however, require the antiquarian zeal of a Flinders Petrie or a Mariette, and even a mere digest of all the antiquities in the 450 miles of the Nile valley through which the traveller bound for Luxor passes, would require several volumes.

Tel-el-Amarna.—Some 20 miles beyond Beni Hassan are the recently discovered rock-tombs of Tel-el-Amarna, the ruins of the city built by the heretical king Amenophis IV. (1400 B.C.), who attempted to change the religion of Egypt. The stopping-place for Tel-el-Amarna is Hadji Kandeel, which is some three miles distant, where donkeys can be obtained for the ride to the ruins.

They were unearthed and scientifically examined by Professor Flinders Petrie in 1892. This excursion is especially attractive to artists on account of the exquisite design and colouring in the painted pavements, the relics of the palaces of King Khu-en-Aten about 2 miles from the Tombs. One floor is in an excellent state of preservation and the colours are remarkably fresh. Near this palace was discovered in 1887 what may be called the Record Office of this enlightened monarch. A large number of bricks were found with the inscription, "The House of the Rolls," which clearly showed the object of the building. Here Dr. Petrie came across a valuable find of the greatest importance to historians and archæologists. It consisted of several hundred clay tablets inscribed with cuneiform characters, comprising despatches to the king from his brother sovereigns of Babylonia and Assyria.

We now reach one of the most picturesque series of reaches in the whole Nile voyage, and here the beautiful dom-palm is first seen. Some 17 miles beyond Tel-el-Amarna are the magnificent precipices of Gebel Abou Feyda. They extend, a precipitous rampart, along the eastern bank of the Nile for nearly a dozen miles. Half concealed in the topmost clefts and fissures of these stupendous precipices can be seen the caves and grottoes where dwelt the celebrated monks and ascetics of Upper Egypt, and here, according to a monastic tradition, Athanasius sought shelter for a time.

Assiout.—This is the capital of Upper Egypt and the largest town between Cairo and Assouan. There is a tolerable hotel (pension 10s.), and the traveller who wishes to be independent of the tourist and mail steamers would find Assiout convenient headquarters for the Gebel Abou Feyda and its tombs, Tel-el-Amarna and other excursions, while Assiout itself is full of interest, and the bazaars are the best in Upper Egypt.

The hills behind the city are honey-combed with tombs, Early Egyptian, Ptolemaic, and Roman, while some of them date from the twelfth dynasty. The principal, known as Stabl Antar, contains some twelfth-dynasty inscriptions and a cartouche of Usertsen I.

Abydos.—Another 100 miles of charming and varied river scenery are passed and we reach Balliana, the starting-place for Abydos. The ruins of the ancient city, the legendary burial-place of Osiris, lie 7 or 8 miles distant across the plain. The chief monument to be seen is the Temple of

Seti I. (father of Rameses the Great) with its magnificent mural decorations and bas-reliefs. This temple is unique as being the only ancient Egyptian roofed temple yet remaining, for of course Denderah, Edfou, and other temples of the Ptolemaic era are modern in comparison. On one of the walls is the famous Stela, known as the **Tablet of Abydos,** a piece of "petrified history" of the greatest value to Egyptologists. It gives a list, with dates of accession, of the first seventy-seven sovereigns of Egypt. In the Temple of Rameses II., a little to the north of the Great Temple, Mr. Banks discovered, in 1818, a fragment (now in the British Museum) of a duplicate Tablet of Abydos.

Between Balliana and Keneh, a distance of some 50 miles, the scenery is pretty, and the vegetation on the banks is rich and abundant, the Nile flowing past fields of Indian corn and sugar-cane, interspersed with plantations of palms.

Temple of Denderah.—Keneh, a town of some 15,000 inhabitants and the chief town of the province, is the stopping-place for the Temple of Denderah, on the opposite shore, a quarter of an hour's ride from the mooring-place. This Temple is one of the most beautiful and best preserved of any in Egypt. It is, however, comparatively modern for Egypt, as it belongs to a late Ptolemaic period.

The walls are almost completely covered with inscriptions and paintings. The famous Zodiac is painted on the ceiling of the portico. It is of Roman workmanship, the date (A.D. 35) being clearly inscribed. The careful observer will notice that most of the symbols of the Greek Zodiac are merely adapted, the *Cancer* being replaced by a Scarab. The well-known portraits of Cleopatra and her son, Cæsarion, are on the end-wall of the exterior. The likeness of the famous queen is purely conventional, the features being of a distinctly Egyptian type, whereas Cleopatra was, of course, of Greek or rather Macedonian, parentage.

Routes.—(1) By mail steamer from Cairo in five and a half days, leaving on Tuesday and Saturday at 9 A.M. There is a restaurant on board. Meals 10 frs. a day.

(2) By rail to Nagh Hamadi and thence by mail steamer. Express in connection with the mail-boats leaves Cairo on Tuesday and Friday at 9.30 P.M. and arrives at Nagh Hamadi the next morning at 10.30. Fare—first-class, £1 : 15 : 9. Sleeping car extra. Steamer fare from Nagh Hamadi to Luxor, £1 : 5 : 9. The steamer is due at Luxor the next evening at 6.25 P.M.

Nagh Hamadi is still the terminus of the Upper Nile river. It was expected that the railway would be completed as far as Luxor by the end of 1897, but up to the present (November 1897) the line has not even reached Keneh.

The tourist steamers of Messrs. Cook and the Thewfikieh being reserved for their own clients, who make the regular three or four weeks' return trip to the First or Second Cataracts, these luxurious steamers are not, unfortunately, available for those travelling independently.

Several weeks' stay at Luxor can, however, be managed in connection with Cook's tourist steamers, by making arrangements at the Cairo office beforehand, passengers being allowed to return by a subsequent steamer *if berths are vacant.* The charge for the trip would be the same whether the passenger goes on to Assouan or not. By this means invalids and others wintering at Luxor can avail themselves of the tourist steamers.

Hotels.—There are three good hotels, but they are apt to be unpleasantly crowded during the height of the season—the months of January and February. The Luxor has accommodation for 140 guests, while the Karnak, a kind of *succursale* of the former, has only room for 60 visitors. These two hotels are virtually under the control of Thomas Cook and Son (Egypt), Limited. The daily charge at each is 13s. (increased to 15s. from 1st January to 15th March). The Luxor is luxuriously appointed and has a large garden. Electric light throughout. Billiard-room, tennis-court, and steam laundry are among the up-to-date features of this hotel. The other hotel, known as the Hotel Thewfikieh, which by many visitors is preferred to the Cook hotels, as being both cheaper and less crowded, belongs to the Thewfikieh Company, and as Messrs. Gaze are the sole agents of this Company their coupons are accepted here. There is a uniform tariff of 12s. a day all through the season.

Church Services.—There is a small Church in the grounds of the Luxor Hotel. Services every Sunday at 8 A.M., 10.30 A.M., and 6.30 P.M.; Chaplain, Rev. H. A. Huleatt (Col. and Cont. Ch. Society). Roman Catholic Church, behind the Thewfikieh Hotel.

English Doctor.—T. W. M. Longmore, M.R.C.S., Luxor Hotel..

English Consular Agent.—Ahmed Mustapha.

Postal Arrangements.—Post and Telegraph Office in the grounds of the Luxor Hotel. The Mail for Cairo leaves every Wednesday, Friday, and Sunday; and there is a delivery every Tuesday, Thursday, and Sunday.

Shops.—*Photographer*—Signor A. Beato. Really artistic photographs can be bought here.

Hairdresser.—Luxor Hotel.

Chemist.—No English chemist, but drugs can be obtained at the native Hospital.

Books.—Guide-books sold at American Mission.

Dealers in Antiquities.—Luxor is notorious for the manufacture of spurious antiquities. The English

Consular agent is, on the whole, the most reliable dealer.

Conveyances. — *Donkeys.* — The donkey-boys usually expect at least 5 piastres for half a day and 10 or 12 piastres for the whole day. This should include baksheesh. There is an understanding among the guides and donkey-boys on either side of the river, which prevents their being taken from Luxor to Thebes or *vice versa.*

Cabs.—There are actually cabs, but they are little used. There is virtually only one drive, viz. to Karnak.

Ferry.—1 piastre.

Guides.—Only inferior guides to be had here. Usual charge 10 to 12 piastres for half a day and 20 piastres for the whole day.

Some time before the steamer arrives at Luxor, the stupendous pylons and obelisks of Karnak, towering above the ruins and palm-groves, warn the tourist that he is approaching the ancient capital of Egypt.

Luxor lies on the east bank of the Nile some 450 miles from Cairo. It is a considerable village, and its inhabitants apparently divide their time between agricultural pursuits and the exploitation of strangers.

The Theban plain afforded a magnificent site for a city, whose ruins show it to have been one of the largest cities in the world, ancient or modern. The mountains which border the Nile Valley recede further from the river, and form a natural amphitheatre, several square miles in extent, divided in the centre by the Nile. Within the area enclosed by these natural ramparts are the innumerable monuments of antiquity which have made Thebes one of the most frequented shrines of tourist culture in the whole world.

History.—The early history of Thebes is obscure, and the name of its founder is not known. It was not till the sixteenth dynasty that Thebes reached its highest point of splendour, and by that period it must have replaced Memphis as the capital of Egypt. Most historians consider that Thebes was founded by colonists from the former city. This seems probable, for as Miss Amelia B. Edwards epigrammatically observes, ancient history in Egypt flows against the stream, and certainly the tide of Egyptian civilisation has always set steadily southwards.

Sight-seeing.—The conscientious sight-seer will certainly be in his element at Luxor. Sight-seeing here is practically the one resource, and it is certainly carried on under the pleasantest conditions. For instance, visitors need not be continually disbursing petty cash for entrance fees, gratuities to attendants, guides, catalogues, etc. In Egypt the single payment of £1 : 0 : 6, the Government tax, franks the tourist not only to these vast treasure-houses of ancient art, but to all the monuments and temples of Upper Egypt.

Itinerary.—A whole winter would scarcely suffice for a thorough investigation of all the Theban ruins, but as nine out of ten visitors are passengers by the tourist or mail steamers, which only allow three days' stay here, the following itinerary may be useful:—

First Day.—The Temples of Luxor and Karnak. The local guides usually recommend a visit to one temple in the morning and the other in the afternoon. As, however, the Luxor Temple is at the threshold of the Luxor Hotel, such a plan involves great waste of time. It can be visited at odd hours. A better plan is for the tourist to take his lunch with him, and devote the greater part of the day to the extensive congeries of temples, usually known as the Great Temple of Karnak.

Second Day.—Ancient Thebes. Chief monuments. (1) Temple of Seti I. (Kurnah); (2) Ramesseum; (3) Colossi (Vocal Memnon); (4) Temple of Rameses III. (Medinet Habû). A hard day's work. An early start should be made. Guides and donkeys plentiful. Charge for both as at Luxor.

Third Day.—The Tombs of the Kings and Queen

Hatshepset's Temple (Dar el Bahari). This is a very fatiguing excursion. A start not later than 6 A.M. should be made, as the heat is usually felt very much.

Temple of Karnak.—The route from Luxor to Karnak lies straight as the crow flies across the plain, along a magnificent avenue nearly two miles long, coeval with the temple, which was once bordered with sphinxes from one end to the other.

"For splendour and magnitude the group of temples at Karnak forms the most magnificent ruin in the world. The temple area is surrounded by a wall of crude brick, in some places still 50 feet in height, along the top of which you may ride for half an hour. The great hall of the great temple measures 170 feet by 329 feet, and the roof, single stones of which weigh 100 tons, is supported by 134 massive columns 60 feet in height.

"The Titanic proportions are the predominant impressions on the part of the tourist, and its architectural and artistic beauties are at first lost in a bewildering sense of bulk and immensity." That the visitor should be almost stupefied by the vastness of scale is scarcely surprising, when we consider that four Notre Dame Cathedrals could be built in the outer walls of the Great Temple, and that the propylon (entrance gateway) equals in breadth alone the length of the nave of many English cathedrals, and in height equals that of the nave of Milan Cathedral.

Almost every sovereign, from Usertsen I. (B.C. 2433) to the Ptolemies, seemed to have regarded the embellishment of this famous shrine or the addition of subsidiary temples as a sacred duty. A glance at Mariette's plans of the original building and that of the Temple, or rather group of temples, in the time of the Ptolemies, shows very clearly the gradual development of the building. To those who take an interest in architecture, the mingling of the various styles during this long period is highly instructive.

Temple of Luxor.—Though the Luxor Temple is of inferior interest, and in the matter of dimensions alone the stupendous fane of Karnak bears the same relation to the Luxor Temple that a European cathedral does to one of its side-chapels, yet anywhere but here it would command respectful attention from the traveller. So great is the wealth of antiquities which strew the site of the ancient Egyptian capital that visitors are, in fact, spoilt for all ruins which are not of surpassing interest. The greater portion of this temple was built by Amen-Hetep III. (*circa* 1400 B.C.) Its most noteworthy feature is a fine obelisk of red granite covered with admirably carved hieroglyphics erected by Rameses

II. Its fellow is familiar to many visitors, as it adorns the Place de la Concorde, Paris.

The antiquities on the western bank, in what is called the Libyan suburb, are more varied and numerous than those on the eastern bank. This portion of the Theban capital served as its cemetery, this Libyan suburb being to Thebes what the necropolis of Sakkarah was to Memphis. This extensive area is one vast museum of antiquities. In fact the saying that in Egypt you have only to scratch the surface to obtain a crop of antiquities applies with special force to the Theban plain.

A few details of the principal monuments follow.

I. Temple of Kurnah.—This temple lies at the extreme northern extremity of the Theban necropolis. It was built by Seti and originally dedicated to Rameses I., and completed by Rameses the Great. This temple was no doubt built as a cenotaph. The Theban temples were intended to serve many purposes. They are, of course, chiefly memorial chapels like the Medici Chapel at Florence or the Spanish Escurial. They also served as a treasury, a kind of muniment room, a library and even a portrait gallery.

II. The Ramasseum.—This is also called by the Greek name Memnonium. This remarkable temple, which "for symmetry of architecture and elegance of sculpture can vie with any other Egyptian monument," is really the mortuary chapel (corresponding to the *mastabas* of Memphis) of Rameses II. In the entrance court a colossal figure of Rameses seated on a throne used to confront the worshipper. The ruins scattered round the pedestal show it to have been the most gigantic figure—to which the Abou Simbel colossi were but statuettes—ever carved in Egypt from a single block of granite. The fact that the granite of this statue would have made three of the great obelisk of Karnak will give some idea of its dimensions. It was probably destroyed by the Persians under Cambyses.

III. The Vocal Memnon.—The most popular, if the word is permissible in connection with these stupendous ruins of an extinct civilisation, of all the Theban monuments are the two colossi which for over three thousand years daily watched the dawn breaking over the Karnak temples. These two alone remain, though they probably formed but the vanguard of a procession of statues which formed the approach to the palace of King Amen-Hetep III. which has now almost entirely disappeared. The most celebrated of these two statues is, of course, the one known as the Vocal Memnon, from a still lingering tradition that it emitted sounds when the sun's rays fell upon it. Many are the theories ventilated by scientists to explain the origin of this legend, for needless to say the statue is mute now, and has remained so, according to the chroniclers, ever since it was repaired in the reign of the Emperor Severus.

The pedestal of the statue is covered with what may be considered testimonials of its musical merits, inscribed in Greek and Latin by visitors from the first century downwards. One of these inscriptions records the visit of the Emperor Hadrian.

IV. Temples of Medinet Habû.—Between the Colossi and the Tombs of the Queens are a remarkable group of monuments known as the Temple of Rameses III., Palace of Rameses III., and Temple of Thothmes III. Rameses' Temple has been recently completely cleared of rubbish. The second court, which in the opinion of Mariette is one of the most precious in any Egyptian temple, is the most interesting feature. The circular columns are very richly painted. The walls are covered with the inevitable battle-scenes.

Adjoining this temple are the ruins of a building which may be regarded as almost unique among the ancient monuments of Egypt, for the internal arrangements show it to have been a palace rather than a temple. Dwelling-houses were almost invariably made of perishable materials, while temples and tombs were intended for eternity. The small temple to the south-east of Rameses' Temple is usually called after Thothmes III. who completed it. The outer courts are of later date than the Sanctuary itself, having been built by one of the Ptolemies. There is a smaller court, which was probably added by Taharka (twenty-fifth dynasty).

It was at Der-el-Medinet, a little south of the Tombs of the Queens, that one of the most important discoveries of papyrus in Egypt was made. Among them was the famous Harris papyrus, now in the British Museum, which gives a very full précis of the reign of Rameses III.

V. Temple of Dar-el-Bahari.—This magnificent pile, which was built by Queen Hatshepset (*circa* 1600 B.C.) is the most splendid of all the noble monuments in the Libyan suburb of Thebes. Its most striking features are admirably described by Miss A. B. Edwards: "Architecturally, it is unlike any other temple in Egypt. It stands at the far end of a deep bay, or natural amphitheatre, formed by the steep limestone cliffs which divide the valley of the Tombs of the Kings from the valley of the Nile. Approached by a pair of obelisks, a pylon gateway, and a long avenue of two hundred sphinxes, the temple consisted of a succession of terraces and flights of steps, rising one above the other, and ending in a maze of colonnades and court-yards uplifted high against the mountain-side. The Sanctuary, or Holy of Holies, to which all the rest was but as an avenue, is excavated in the face of the cliff some five hundred feet above the level of the Nile. The novelty of the plan is so great that one cannot help wondering whether it was suggested to the architect by the nature of the ground, or whether it was in any degree a reminiscence of strange edifices seen in far distant lands. It bears, at all events, a certain resemblance to the terraced temples of Chaldea."

Queen Hatshepset (or Hatasu) who was the daughter of Thothmes I., and wife as well as half-sister of Thothmes II., seems to have been the Cleopatra of the eighteenth dynasty, and has been happily termed the "Queen Elizabeth of Egyptian history."

The unearthing and restoration of the ruins of this great temple has been one of the most important works carried out within recent years by the Egypt Exploration Fund. The work had occupied them four successive winters, and was only completed in the season of 1896-97. The discoveries brought to light during this long and systematic excavation are of the greatest antiquarian and historical value. One of the most significant was the discovery of a large hall in which was a large stone altar, the only one discovered in Egypt. The altar is dedicated to the queen's father, Harmachis. It is curious that Hatshepset's cartouche is rarely found perfect. It is usually more or less erased, probably through the jealousy of her successor, Thothmes III.

VI. The Tombs of the Kings.—These should be reserved for a whole day's excursion. They are hewn out of the living rock in the precipitous mountains which form the background of the Theban necropolis. The contrast between the fertile plain and these gloomy gorges is very striking, and the name, "Valley of Death," which has been given to these dreary and desolate defiles, is happily chosen. The kings of the nineteenth and twentieth dynasties were buried here, though the royal mummies had been removed to Dar-el-Bahari about 966 B.C. to secure them against pillage, a precaution, we are reminded by the presence of the mummies at Ghizeh, quite ineffectual against excavating savants and antiquarians. Several of the best sarcophagi are distributed amongst continental museums—the sarcophagus of Rameses III. is in the Louvre, the lid in the Fitz-William Museum, Cambridge, while the mummy itself is in the Cairo Museum. Though the chief interest of these tombs is therefore wanting, yet the tombs themselves are worthy of thorough examination. The principle of construction is somewhat similar to that of the Assouan tombs. They consist of long inclined tunnels intersected by mortuary chambers which in some cases burrow into the heart of the rock for four or five hundred feet. "Belzoni's Tomb" (No. 17) is one of the show ones. Here was buried Seti I., father of Rameses the Great. The magnificent sarcophagus is one of the chief treasures of the Soane Museum in Lincoln's Inn Fields. It is nine feet in length, carved out of one block of oriental alabaster. This sarcophagus was discovered by Belzoni in the year 1817, and purchased by Sir John Soane from Mr. Salt in 1824 for the sum of £2000.

According to Strabo there are forty of these royal tombs, but the labours of the Government officials have not yet succeeded in bringing to light more than twenty-five of these sepulchres. Scarcely more than half of the tombs which have been opened are included, however, in the ordinary dragoman's programme. The walls of the corridors and of the mortuary chamber are covered with extracts from the *Book of the Dead*, and paintings which show skilful and elaborate draughtmanship.

For the practical purpose of getting some idea of the confusing topography of the site of Ancient Thebes as well as for the æsthetic enjoyment of an incomparable view, one of the peaks of the mountain barrier which mounts guard over the Tombs of the Kings should be climbed.

III.—FROM LUXOR TO THE SECOND CATARACT

Routes from Luxor to Assouan.—(1) *By Mail Steamer*, which leaves Luxor on Thursday and Sunday at 7 P.M., arriving at Assouan at 10 A.M. on Saturday and Tuesday respectively. Single first-class fare, £2 : 8 : 6 (exclusive of meals). Passengers returning by the same steamer can make the ship their headquarters without extra charge during the stay of the steamer at Assouan.

The only temples which can be visited by passengers are Esneh and Edfou (on the return journey only), while passengers by the tourist steamers have facilities of visiting also the ancient Quarries of Silsileh, the Temple of Kom-Ombo, and the Grottoes of El-Kab.

Though the mail service is remarkably cheap, it can only be recommended to those who are willing to forgo intermediate sight-seeing, for the hurried visits of little more than an hour or so to each temple is decidedly unsatisfactory.

(2) *By Tourist Steamer.*—Messrs. Cook and Son and the Thewfikieh Company. For dates and fares see pages 171-174. Only passengers who make the whole trip from Cairo are taken, for there is no intermediate booking.

A few miles south of Luxor, on the west bank, are the uninteresting fragments of the Ptolemaic Temple of Erment, but there is nothing to attract the ordinary tourist till the beautiful Temple of Esneh, some twenty-five miles further south, is reached.

Temple of Esneh.—The colours of the paintings which cover the walls of the Hall of Columns are apparently as fresh and brilliant as when they were laid on. This is due to the preservative qualities of the desert sand, by which the whole temple was buried for centuries, till Mehemet Ali's workmen cleared away the sand from this part of it. The columns are very beautiful and are richly decorated. They are all of a different pattern. A very strong Greek influence is seen in the treatment of the mural decorations.

Temple of Edfou.—Some thirty miles above Esneh, a few minutes' ride from the landing-place, is the most perfectly preserved temple in Egypt—Edfou. Its general features are very similar to those of Denderah, and it is planned on a scale almost rivalling in magnificence some of the Pharaonic temples of Ancient Thebes, the two pylons being 112 feet high. The last hall serves as a shrine to Horus, the god to whom the temple is dedicated. The pylons are covered with battle-scenes.

One of the corridors is devoted to a complete series of sporting pictures, and the humorous realism shown in some of these is amusing. For instance, in a picture of a hippopotamus hunt, the clumsy harpooner has speared one of the attendants by mistake!

Mariette's labours have mainly contributed to the unearthing and preservation of this gem among Ptolemaic monuments. When he entered upon the work of excavation in 1864 it was buried almost to the cornices in mounds of rubbish, and a great part of the roof was covered with native huts and stables.

Silsileh Quarries.—Two or three hours after leaving Edfou the scenery becomes wilder. The river here flows through a stupendous gorge formed by the sandstone precipices of Silsileh. These were extensively quarried by the Egyptians from a very early period. Like the Quarries of Assouan and Tûra (near Helouan) they were used in Pharaonic times for building temples and other monuments.

Temple of Kom-Ombo.—Between Silsileh and Assouan the only temple visited by the ordinary tourist is Kom-Ombo (556 miles from Cairo), which stands on a precipitous plateau overlooking the Nile. It is one of the latest temples restored, or rather cleared of sand, by M. de Morgan. Though small compared to the magnificent edifices of Luxor and Karnak, it is one of the most beautifully-proportioned temples in Upper Egypt.

The scenery in the fifty miles stretch between Silsileh and Assouan is bold and picturesque. Rock everywhere gives place to sand, and instead of fields of maize and wheat the chief vegetation are groves of palms, mimosa, and castor-oil shrub in the ravines and crevices of the precipices which border the river. "The limestone and sandstone ranges which hem in the Nile Valley from Cairo to Silsileh, give place to granite, porphyry, and basalt. The ruined convents and towers which crown the hills might almost cheat us into the belief that we were afloat on the Rhine or the Moselle, but for the tropical character of the scenery."

Assouan.—The modern town stands well above the river, and has an imposing appearance from the river, the quay being lined with Government buildings, hotels, and shops. Assouan itself has few remains of the extinct civilisation of Egypt, most of the antiquities being Saracenic or late Roman. It affords, however, comfortable headquarters for those wishing to explore the chief sights of the neighbourhood—the islands of Philæ and Elephantine, Grenfell Tombs, the ancient Quarries, and the First Cataract.

As a health resort of the future, Assouan must be reckoned with. Though the furthest outpost of invalid colonisation in Egypt, distant nearly six hundred miles from the capital, it is fairly well provided with the requirements of invalids, including a good but expensive hotel, a resident doctor and chaplain, English vice-consul, chemist, and post and telegraph office with deliveries and departures three times a week.

Philæ.—The Island of Philæ is the chief feature of interest at Assouan. Though a mere rock, barely a quarter of a mile long, it is thickly covered with ruins of Ptolemaic temples and monuments, and is, perhaps, the most beautiful as well as the smallest historic island in the world. The scenery about here is very striking and impressive—in fact, "The approach to Philæ" has been rendered almost as familiar to the arm-chair traveller, by means of innumerable sketches, as the Pyramids or the Sphinx.

Though the temples are Ptolemaic and of slight historic value, for picturesqueness of form and surroundings they are scarcely equalled by the ancient Theban temples. The most striking features of the Great Temple are the colonnade of thirty-two columns, and the massive towers of the pylon, each 120 feet wide and 60 feet high. Traces still remain of the vivid and varied colouring, for, according to the canons of art then prevailing, the shafts and capitals were painted. There are other courts and colonnades in the Temple, which seems indeed rather a congeries of temples, like the Great Temple of Karnak, than a single building. The walls are covered with sculptures in low relief.

Another beautiful ruin is the old Temple of Osiris, which, like the palace of Charles V. in the Alhambra, never possessed a roof. It is known to tourists as Pharaoh's Bed, so called because of a fancied resemblance to a colossal four-post bed.

The island is thickly strewn with ruins of other temples dedicated either to Isis, Osiris, or Horus, the tutelary triad of the island. In fact, Philæ was the last refuge of this cult, a Greek inscription showing that these gods were worshipped here down to 453 A.D.

The Nilometer consists merely of some steps leading down to the river, with the cubits for marking the rise of the Nile engraved on the walls on either side. There is a more elaborate nilometer on Elephantine Island.

Philæ is just above the Cataract, and is most conveniently reached from Shellal, the terminus of the new military railway from Assouan, built to "turn" the Cataract. There is a morning train from Assouan, returning at noon. Return fare, first-class, 20 piastres.

Elephantine Island lies opposite Assouan. The Nilometer here is worth visiting, but the scanty remains of two eighteenth-dynasty temples (destroyed early in the present century) are interesting only to archæologists.

The Rock Tombs.—The Tombs which, according to the absurd practice which prevails in Egypt of labelling remains after the name of the discoverer, are popularly known as Grenfell's Tombs, have only been partially explored. They were excavated in the cliffs of the western bank of the Nile. The excavations of these rock shrines were begun by General Grenfell in 1887. In some respects they resemble the tombs of Beni Hassan, but it is only at Assouan that we see traces of the striking methods of transporting the bodies of the dead. It is a kind of slide cut out from the face of the almost perpendicular cliff, and on each side are remains of the steps for the bearers who drew up the mummy from the river.

The most striking tomb is that of Ra-Nub-Ko-Necht, a high official of Amen-Em-Hat I. a sovereign of the twelfth dynasty, but it is generally—perhaps excusably, in view of the cumbrous designation of its tenant—known as Grenfell's Tomb. The entrance to this tomb is impressive from the startling contrasts, and perhaps was intended to produce a dramatic effect on the spectator.

The Ancient Quarries.—Scarcely a mile from the town are the famous granite quarries of Syene, from which was hewn the stone for most of the famous obelisks and other monoliths of the early Egyptian kings. In fact, certain inscriptions show that even in the sixth dynasty stone was quarried here for Egyptian temples and sarcophagi. An obelisk, nearly 100 ft. in length, entirely detached on three sides from the rock, may be seen *in situ*, as well as unfinished columns, sarcophagi, etc., which show that Syene in the time of the Pharaohs was not only a quarry, but what we should nowadays describe as a monumental mason's stone-yard.

The First Cataract. — Cataract is rather a misnomer, for there is no distinct cascade or waterfall. The First Cataract really consists of a series of rapids and eddies, extending from the Island of Sehel, just above Assouan, to Mahatta, below Philæ. There is considerable excitement, but practically no danger in the ascent of the Cataract, but for an ordinary dahabeah, the cost of the undertaking is heavy, seldom amounting with baksheesh to less than £10.

Route from Assouan to the Second Cataract.—Messrs. Cook's first-class tourist steamer, *Prince Abbas* (with accommodation for forty-two passengers only), leaves Shellal every Monday from 27th December in connection with the Cairo-Assouan service for Wady Halfa. The trip there and back takes eight days. Fare, which includes all expenses except wine, £30. But those who have already travelled to Assouan under Messrs. Cook's arrangements pay only £23.

This service practically replaces the Government mail stern-wheelers. These still run, but there is rarely accommodation for civilian passengers. These are used chiefly for troops and mails.

The voyage can also be very cheaply done by one of the *native* dahabeahs (very inferior, of course, to the modern Cairo dahabeahs), which could be hired at Shellal for the fortnight's trip to Wady Halfa and back, including three or four days' stay at Wady Halfa, for about £16 or £17 (including pilot and baksheesh). This kind of conveyance might be recommended to a party of three or four artists or sportsmen who are prepared for very rough accommodation, but it would be necessary for one of the party to speak and understand a little Arabic, and to have had some experience of independent Nile travel. An ordinary dragoman, engaged at

Cairo, would probably decline to travel in such a wretched craft.

The 200 miles voyage to Wady Halfa is most interesting, and should not be omitted by any Nile traveller who can afford the time. The scenic and historic attractions are many, and to visit the Temple of Abou Simbel alone is worth the long 800 miles voyage from Cairo.

The chief attractions are admirably summed up in Messrs. Cook's Nile pamphlet. "They include the unrivalled Gorge of Kalabsheh, where the great river is narrowed between giant granite rocks; the mountain fortress of Ibraim—the Gibraltar of the Nile; Korosko, the old starting-point of the caravans for Khartoum; the historic battlefield of Toski; the temples of Dendoor, Dakkeh, Derr, and Abou Simbel."

Want of space will prevent even the briefest description of any of these monuments except the famous rock-hewn temples of Abou Simbel, which, in the estimation of most travellers, are only exceeded in historical and antiquarian interest by the Pyramids of Ghizeh and the Theban Temples.

Scenery.—The scenery of Nubia—for geographically Nubia begins at the First Cataract, though politically the Egyptian frontier now (November 1897) extends to Berber—differs considerably from that of Egypt, being bolder and more varied. For the first hundred miles or so "a glaring reddish desert, studded with black pointed rocks, and with narrow strips of green, and palm-trees by the side, make up scenery which is more beautiful and diversified than in Egypt." Afterwards, from Ibraim to Wady Halfa the scenery is more of the desert type, and is comparatively monotonous.

Temples of Abou Simbel.—These wonderful rock-temples (known to the travellers of the last century as Isampoul), which lie on the western bank close to the river, some 50 miles south of Wady Halfa, must impress the most matter-of-fact traveller, however sated with the monuments of ancient grandeur and wealth at Karnak and Thebes.

The Great Temple is a superb conception of Egypt's greatest sovereign. Rameses simply took a vast hill-side and carved a temple out of its heart, while on the immense façade, 120 feet long and 100 feet high, he placed the "four immortal warders, his own royal likeness four times repeated." These colossal statues are nearly 70 feet high, and the forefinger of each is a yard long.

The temple is so orientated that on one day of the year, probably on the day of the dedication, at sunrise one shaft of light pierces the darkness of the outer and inner halls, and "falls like living fire on the shrine itself, the effect being overwhelming in its mystery and awe."

To the historian Abou Simbel is mainly of importance as containing a long chronicle in stone of Rameses the Great, in which he describes the great work he has carried out in his temple at Thebes. Here are also inscribed the history in great detail of the king's famous campaign in Asia. This he evidently considered his greatest military achievement, for it is inscribed on the walls of the Theban Ramasseum and at Abydos.

Temple of Hathor.—A little to the north of the Great Temple is the small Temple of Hathor, with the façade also cut out of the perpendicular face of the cliff. This is a memorial chapel dedicated to Queen Nefert-Ari, the favourite wife of Rameses II. Those who have travelled in India will be reminded, by the beautiful legend of the mutual love of husband and wife inscribed on the façade, of the famous Taj Mahal at Agra. The king writes, "Rameses, the Strong in Truth, the Beloved of Amen, made this divine abode for his royal wife, Nefert-Ari, whom he loves."

Wady Halfa.—Between Abou Simbel and the old frontier, Wady Halfa, the scenery is dreary and tame, and there are scarcely any ruins to break the monotony of the voyage.

The one lion of Wady Halfa is the famous **Pulpit Rock** of Abusir some 300 ft. high, with the incomparable view of the Nile and the Libyan Desert. This rock is a veritable "visitors' list" in stone, and the names of almost every traveller of note has been inscribed here. The dragoman firmly believes that Moses' name might once have been seen among the graven autographs, though he is careful to add, in order to take the wind out of the sails of the sceptical tourist, "that it has long been worn away!" At all events, Belzoni's name is to be seen there, high up on the rock, and, still higher, Gordon's.

There are few views which impress the spectator so much as the grand prospect from the platform which forms the summit of the rock. Looking down on one side is the rushing and eddying Nile, studded with black shining rocks dividing the river into endless channels—these are the rapids known as the Second Cataract—the eastern bank is a wild jumble of black rocks and boulders, the debris brought down in high flood. The absence of any sign of habitation intensifies the sensation of wild desolation and awful grandeur. In the distance misty blue mountains conceal Dongola, some 150 miles south. Turning round and looking westward, the view is even more impressive.

IV.—THE NILE AS A HEALTH RESORT.[1]

MANY English people who are accustomed to spend the winter in one of the relatively cheap towns of the two Rivieras, are often deterred from wintering in the undeniably superior climate of Egypt by the expense of the journey and the high cost of living in Cairo. The City of the Caliphs is, no doubt, one of the most expensive health resorts in the world, not only owing to the high charges of its splendidly equipped hotels, but to its great vogue as a fashionable cosmopolitan winter city. People are, however, beginning to realise that Cairo is not necessarily Egypt, and indeed as a health resort pure and simple, as I have shown in a previous chapter, it is by no means to be recommended unreservedly.

Egypt, however, offers a choice of some four or five health resorts besides Cairo, viz. Helouan, Mena

[1] The greater part of this chapter is taken from an article contributed to *The North American Review*.

House (Pyramids), Luxor, Assouan, and the Nile. As for Assouan it should perhaps be regarded, in spite of its resident doctor and chaplain, and good hotel accommodation, a potential rather than an actual climatic health station. The objection to Luxor is, that its hotels are often over-crowded during the season, and the constant coming and going of the Nile tourists makes the place noisy and bustling. Helouan is apt to be dull and depressing. Mena House, at the Pyramids, is undeniably expensive, and the fashionable society element is too obtrusive to make it desirable winter quarters for the invalid.

The Nile as a health resort suffers from none of these drawbacks, and the climate of the Upper Nile and Nubia is undeniably superior to that of Lower Egypt. The Egyptian climate has, however, been sufficiently described in the chapter "CAIRO AS A HEALTH RESORT."

The fullest benefit from the Egyptian climate is gained from a prolonged Nile voyage, while the asceptícity — word beloved by the faculty — of the atmosphere is greater than at Luxor or Assouan. Then the Nile itself is more equable in temperature than its banks. On the other hand, invalid passengers on these miniature pleasure-barges—for one is bound to admit that the lines of the dahabeah approximate more nearly to those of a Thames house-boat than a yacht—are not well protected from cold winds, which makes some physicians look askance on dahabeah trips for persons with delicate lungs. Besides, though the actual extremes of temperature are less on the river than in the desert, the difference is felt more by patients than when protected by the thick walls of an hotel. It is curious, too, that the cold at night seems to increase the further one goes south. These constitute the only real drawbacks to dahabeahs for delicate persons.

Formerly the only orthodox way of doing the Nile voyage was by means of these native sailing-boats, but the costliness of this means of locomotion practically confined it to the English milord. Of late years the wholesome competition of the great tourist agencies has brought about a general reduction in the rents of these pleasure craft. With a party of four or five the inclusive cost of the two months' voyage to Assouan and back need not exceed £110 to £120 per head—granting, of course, that the organiser of the trip knows the river, has had some experience of Nile travel, and is able to hold his own with his dragoman.

For the health-seeker as well as the mere holiday-maker the dahabeah voyage is still the ideal method of spending a winter in Egypt. In short, this form of the New Yachting is to the invalid what the pleasure yachting cruise—the latest development of co-operative travel—is to the ordinary tourist, Though independent, the traveller is not isolated, and can always get in touch with civilisation as represented by the tourist steamers and mail-boats, which virtually patrol the Nile from Cairo to Wady Halfa. Then for the first 350 miles he is never more than a few hours' sail from a railway station, the line for the greater part of its length running along the Nile banks, and almost every station is a telegraph office as well. English doctors and chaplains are to be found throughout the season at the chief goals of the voyage—Luxor and Assouan, while, in cases of emergency, the services of the medical men attached to the tourist steamers are usually available.

The voyage is eminently restful without being dull or monotonous. In fact, the Nile being the great highway of traffic for Nubia and Upper Egypt to Cairo and Alexandria there is constant variety, and the river traffic affords plenty of life and movement. One constantly passes the picturesque trading dahabeahs gliding along with their enormous lateen sails, the artistic effect heightened by contrast with a trim, modern steam-dahabeah—as incongruous a craft as a gondola turned into a steam-launch, and utterly opposed to the traditions of Nile travel—too reminiscent perhaps of Cookham Reach or Henley. The banks of the river, quite apart from the temples and monuments of antiquity, are also full of interest for the observant voyager, who may congratulate himself on the superiority of his lot to his less fortunate invalid brethren wintering on the Riviera, and "killing time till time kills them"—chained for the greater part of the day, perhaps, to the hotel-balcony or villa garden at Mentone, Monte Carlo, or San Remo.

Delightful "bits" for the sketch-book are constantly to be met with. At almost every village—and many are passed in a day's sail—native women may be seen filling their earthen jars with water, and carrying them on their heads with all the ease and grace of a Capriote girl. Jabbering gamins are driving down the banks the curious little buffaloes to water. Every now and then we pass a shadoof tended by a fellah with skin shining like bronze, relieving his toil with that peculiar wailing chant, which seems to the imaginative listener like the echo of the Israelites' cry under their taskmasters wafted across the centuries. The shrill note of a steamer-whistle puts to flight these poetical fancies, and one of Messrs. Cook's tourist steamers, looking for all the world like a Hudson or Mississipi river-steamer, dashes past at twelve knots an hour, her deck crowded with tourists more or less noisily appreciative of the Nile scenery. However, this incongruous and insistent note of modernity is fleeting enough. Has not the appointed goal, some fifty miles or so higher up, to be reached by dusk, or the arrangements of the whole Nile itinerary, and the plans of hundreds of tourists, would be utterly upset?

Animal life, to say nothing of bird-life, is far more abundant than in Italy or France. Flocks of pelicans stud the sand-banks, and white paddy birds may be seen busily engaged in fishing, while brilliantly decked kingfishers, graceful hoopoes, sun-birds, and crested larks, to say nothing of our familiar friends the swifts, swallows, and water-wagtails, are flitting about over the water. Occasionally a keen-sighted traveller will get a glimpse of an eagle or vulture.

Reptiles are represented by various kinds of lizards and the chameleons. Crocodiles, of course, are never seen below the First Cataract, though the monitor lizard, often mistaken for this reptile, is occasionally seen, and the unwary tourist occasionally has stuffed specimens palmed off upon him as young crocodiles by the wily Egyptian.

The Egyptian sunsets are, of course, famous, but nowhere, except perhaps on the Red Sea, or Gulf of Suez, are the atmospheric effects so brilliant and striking as on the Nile. Their unique character is sometimes coldly explained by the learned as being due to the excessive dryness of the atmosphere, and the haze of impalpable dust arising from the dried deposit of the annual inundation. Only the pen of a Ruskin could at all adequately describe the extraordinarily beautiful atmospheric effects of the Egyptian dawns and sunsets. The whole sky, from the zenith to the horizon, becomes a dome of gold shading off into crimson, purple, and opalescent hues, while the glassy mirror of the Nile gleams like molten metal. This splendour is followed by the soft sheen of the zodiacal light. Perhaps of all the wonderful scenic effects of the Nile this almost miraculous afterglow is the most impressive. Only those with a true "feeling for colour" can properly appreciate it, for to attempt to portray it, either with pen or pencil, would be futile. These startling effects may be called miraculous because inexplicable. In the tropics, as everyone knows, there is no after-glow—"The sun's rim dips, the stars rush out; at one stride comes the dark," sings Coleridge's "Ancient Mariner." Only a scientist can explain why in Egypt, on the very threshold of the Tropic of Cancer, the sunset's afterglow lasts thrice as long as it does elsewhere in the same zone.

But the Nile sunsets are among the commonplaces

of impressions of travellers, and, after all, painters will tell you that gorgeousness is not the dominant note of the scenery. The great fascination of Nile scenery consists in its simplicity—a flowing river, desert sands, a ruined temple, an isolated palm-tree, with the human interest afforded by a fellah working at his shadoof, are the sole materials of the painter. In short, on the Nile, as Mr. H. D. Traill aptly observes, you get the broadest artistic effects produced by the slenderest means.

Life on a dahabeah has, in short, many of the advantages of a luxuriously appointed yacht, without its inseparable and obvious drawbacks. There are no storms, and indeed no calms, for a northern wind blows as regularly as a trade wind almost continuously during the winter and spring months. You stop where you please and as long as you please, without a thought of harbour dues, or anxiety as to the holding capacity of the anchorage. You can spend your time sketching, reading, or dozing, with a little shooting to give a fillip to the perpetual *dolce far niente.* You can explore ruined temples and other ancient monuments at your leisure, without the disquieting reflections that the Theban ruins, or the Ptolemaic Temples of Philæ, must be "done" in a certain time or the tourist steamer will proceed on its unalterable itinerary without you. Finally, when tired of this perpetual picnic, you can enjoy for a few days the banal delights of a first-class modern hotel at Luxor or Assouan.

Such is life on a dahabeah, but alas this epicurean existence is not for the ordinary sun-worshipper. As I have shown, it is a particularly costly form of holiday-making, though the expense is often much exaggerated.

Practical Hints on Dahabeahs.—The valuable advice given in Murray's *Handbook for Egypt* on the hiring of dahabeahs, may be supplemented by the following hints. If the hirer is a novice in Nile travel, or is not prepared to take a considerable amount of trouble, it will be better to hire the vessel through Messrs. Cook or Gaze direct.

Messrs. Cook have the best selection of modern dahabeahs. The larger ones, for nine or ten passengers, have steel hulls, and are most luxuriously appointed, with large bath-room, refrigerator, and even a piano! The great advantage of hiring one of these miniature floating hotels from this firm, is that a constant supply of fresh meat, fruit, vegetables, milk, etc., can be had from the tourist steamers and the farms at Luxor without extra charge. The inclusive charges, which vary considerably according to the number of the passengers and the type of dahabeah, are from £60 to £100 a month per head.

These charges, considering the high degree of comfort assured, cannot be considered dear.

It must be remembered, however, that when hiring one of these luxurious crafts from this famous firm, though the hirer is relieved of all worry and responsibility, he will not be so likely to feel himself "captain on his own quarter-deck," as he would if he hired direct from a private owner. In the latter case, it is decidedly an advantage to make a separate contract with the dragoman for the catering of the passengers, and another contract with the owner direct for the hire of the dahabeah with fittings (which should be specifically set out), the wages of the reis (sailing-master) and crew, and any charge for ascending the First Cataract. If, however, the contract is made with the dragoman solely, then take pains to ascertain that the boat is not the dragoman's property, or the temporary owner may find it difficult to maintain his authority, and besides the dragoman will naturally be inclined to be too careful of his craft, and will raise difficulties about shooting the cataracts or sailing at night. In short, the hirer will possibly find himself at as great a disadvantage as a yacht-owner in a foreign cruise who has neglected to have himself registered as master in the yacht's papers.

Besides, the ordinary Nile dragoman is absurdly

conservative, and is generally opposed to anything which offends against his notions of orthodox Nile travel. For instance, unless the hirer takes up an independent attitude from the first, the dragoman may raise objections to stopping for the purpose of sight-seeing when there is a fair wind, and may try to put off visits to the monuments till the return voyage. He is also averse to halting for any ruins which are not in the regulation itinerary.

As to the time occupied in the voyage from Cairo to Assouan and back, with favourable winds it can be managed in seven or eight weeks. But this might only allow very few days for Luxor and Assouan. Besides, anything like hurry is utterly foreign to the traditions of Nile voyaging, and three months would not be found too long for this trip; or longer, if it be continued to the Second Cataract. It must be remembered, too, that if the contract is for three months, the cost would be considerably less relatively than for two months. It would be better to allow three months and, wind and *water* permitting, make — unless late in the season — Wady Halfa the goal, for, of course, late in the spring the Cataract at Assouan is impassible for dahabeahs drawing much water.

For those who are wintering in Egypt for their health, there can be no question of the superiority of the dahabeah over all other modes of Nile travel. To many, however, the great expense is an insuperable drawback, and for these a series of voyages in the well-found and well-equipped tourist steamers of Messrs. Cook or the Thewfikieh Company, will be found a tolerable substitute. In fact, Messrs. Cook specially cater for this class of tourist, by offering special terms to passengers making three consecutive trips on the basis of three voyages at the price of two. By this plan passengers can make three voyages from Cairo to Assouan and back for £100, the fare including board on the steamer during the few days' stay at Cairo between the voyages; thus nine weeks can be spent on the Nile at a less cost than a stay for the same period at a fashionable Cairo hotel. Considering that the mileage covered by these voyages amounts to about 3500 miles—equal to the distance from London to Alexandria by sea—it is not surprising that this remarkably economical method of undertaking what is supposed to be one of the most expensive of river trips in the globe-trotter's itinerary is becoming popular.

As for the mail-steamers, which afford comfortable and economical accommodation for the ordinary traveller, they are, of course, utterly unsuited for delicate persons.

PART IV

POLITICAL AND ANTIQUARIAN

I.—THE REGENERATION OF EGYPT

EGYPT, in view of its wealth of antiquities and artistic relics, is no doubt of the highest importance to the antiquarian traveller. Regarded, however, as a community or modern state, Egypt of to-day holds a low rank among semi-civilised countries. There is some reason for the complaint of some modern historians, that western minds seem to lose all sense of proportion and historic perspective when describing this Land of Paradox. Yet, regarded internally it is but a tenth-rate territory, with an acreage less than that of Belgium, and a population hardly more numerous than is possessed by Ireland.

At the same time, one cannot deny the great importance of Egypt in spite of its small acreage and population. This, no doubt, is fictitious, due partly to its peculiar geographical position, which makes it the great highway between the Eastern and Western hemispheres, and partly to its climate, which has converted it into the great winter residence and playground of civilised nations.

The attitude of England, in its policy of Egyptian intervention since the Arabi revolt, seemed at first simple enough. It was natural that the British Government supposed that their task, when France in 1882 threw all responsibility for Egypt on their hands, was merely to crush a military rising. Only actual experience taught England that the rebellion was a very small matter, and that the real difficulty lay in the utter rottenness of the whole fabric of government. Naturally then the pledges England made, being based on a total misapprehension, were impossible of fulfilment. But to the spirit of these pledges England has been faithful. Besides, it is indisputable that England has derived no pecuniary benefit from her occupation of Egypt. As a matter of fact, among the foreign employés in the Egyptian Civil Service there are nearly twice as many of French or Italian nationality as English.

In order to appreciate the significance of the great reforms carried out by Great Britain, the maze of difficulties, both internal and external, she had to contend against, when she unwillingly entered upon the rôle of reformer, must not be lost sight of. Her attitude towards Europe is indicated by the famous despatch of Lord Granville addressed to the Powers in January 1883.

"Although for the present," says that document,

"a British force remains in Egypt for the preservation of public tranquillity, Her Majesty's Government are desirous of withdrawing it as soon as the state of the country and the organisation of proper means for the maintenance of the Khedive's authority will admit of it. In the meantime, the position in which Her Majesty's Government are placed towards His Highness imposes upon them the duty of giving advice with the object of securing that the order of things to be established shall be of a satisfactory character, and possess the elements of stability and progress."

This constitutes one of the famous "pledges of withdrawal" with which England is twitted, in season and out of season, by the French press. In fact, in a leading French journal published at Alexandria, these pledges are *daily* printed in a prominent position on the front page!

Three courses were open to England in 1883—annexation, an absolute protectorate, or temporary occupation. This latter course, which was virtually a veiled or disguised protectorate, was finally adopted, as is indicated by Lord Granville's despatch quoted above. This policy was, of course, a compromise, and like most compromises is open to criticism.

"It is certain that, if we had grasped the Egyptian nettle boldly, if we had proclaimed from the first our intention of exercising even for a time that authority which, as a matter of fact, we do exercise, we could have made the situation not only much more endurable for the Egyptians, but much easier for ourselves. Had we seen our way to declaring even a temporary protectorate, we might have suspended the capitulations, if we could not have got rid of them altogether, as France has done in Tunis."

As for the attitude of the French Government, it is natural enough that France should feel some resentment at England holding the position in Egypt among all European nations that she herself once held, and foolishly resigned, when in 1882 she shirked at the last moment and left England to "face the music" alone. In short, logically, France is mainly answerable for the British continued occupation in Egypt. But yet it must be allowed that France has many reasons for being hurt and disappointed, considering the enormous value of her services to Egypt in the past.

It was France who supported Egypt in her struggle for independence from Turkey, when all the other Powers were against her, and when by this opposition they prevented that independence from becoming complete. It was to France that Mehemet Ali turned for aid in his attempts to civilise Egypt, as he understood the meaning of civilisation. "For something like half a century, French lawyers, French engineers, French men of learning, were engaged in doing their best—often under most discouraging circumstances—to deluge Egypt with the fruits of European culture."

It is necessary, however, to look at the other side of the question. France has no doubt been of great service to this erstwhile "distressful country," but her services are counterbalanced by her tendency to exploit and make money out of Egypt, which seems to have been a cardinal principle of her Egyptian policy, from the death of Mehemet Ali down to 1882.

The more important reforms and improvements carried out by England during this virtual protectorate of the country, are summarised below. They may conveniently be divided according to the great State departments, the Army, Finance, Justice and Police, Public Works, and Education.

1.—The Army.—The most pressing was the remodelling of the discredited and useless Egyptian Army. In this case, however, "mending" emphatically meant "ending," and this was effected by the famous laconic decree of December 1882—"The Egyptian army is disbanded." But Sir Evelyn Wood, to whom the task of creating a new army was entrusted, did not despair of converting the fellah into a useful fighting machine, and his faith in what looked very poor material has in the two last campaigns been thoroughly justified.

The fellaheen are no doubt wanting in initiative power and individuality, but when intelligently led they fight well. In fact, as is the case with Turkish soldiers, good leadership is simply everything in the field. Then the Egyptian soldiers are not wanting in the useful quality of insensibility to danger, which is a fair substitute for true courage. A native army was, however, all very well, but it required to be "stiffened" by English troops. Besides, it was obvious that without the moral support afforded by the presence of an English army of occupation, it would be hopeless to carry out any lasting projects of reform. The position of the British army of occupation is, no doubt, anomalous in the extreme.

The British troops have, of course, no sort of status in the country. They are not the soldiers of the Khedive, or foreign soldiers invited by the Khedive, They are not the soldiers of the protecting power, since there is in theory no protecting power. Ostensibly their presence is an accident, and their character that of simple visitors. But its value as a fighting force does not, of course, constitute the real importance and meaning of the British army of occupation. It is as the outward and visible sign of the predominance of British influence, that that army is such an important element in the present situation; and its moral effect is out of all proportion to its actual strength.

2. **Finance.**—In financial reforms the Khedive's English advisers had a far more difficult task than in those connected with the army. They were virtually in the power of the *Caisse* which represented the bond-holders, and in the interest of Egypt's creditors the public services were starved. A certain fixed sum (about £6,000,000) was annually allowed for all the expenses of government. Even if there were a surplus in the Treasury after the payment of this sum and the interest, the country only partially benefited, for half of any extra revenue was to be devoted to the reduction of the debt.

Such was Egypt's financial position when England entered upon the task of bringing the revenue and the expenditure into a state of stable equilibrium. The results have exceeded the most sanguine expectations. The chief features of the new fiscal policy are a more equitable distribution of the taxes, the suppression of the *corvée* (the forced labour of the peasants for the dredging and repair of the canals), greater outlay on reproductive works, and less expenditure on "non-effective" objects. All this has been accomplished without any increase in the annual expenditure.

"Two great factors have combined to bring about the financial recuperation of Egypt: the prevention of waste on the part of the administration, and the development of the productive powers of the country. As far as the prevention of waste is concerned, the first essential was a proper system of accounts. Accounts are the foundation of finance. There was nothing more fatal in the financial chaos of the days of Ismail than the manner in which the private property of the Khedive was jumbled up with the property of the State. This mischievous confusion was put an end to when Ismail's vast estates were surrendered to his creditors, and a regular Civil List substituted for the multifarious revenues which at one time flowed into the coffers of the Government of Egypt."

The material wealth of the country is far from being exhausted, and if proper measures are taken to economise Egypt's potential productiveness, Egypt might yet attain a considerable degree of prosperity. It is all a question of water. The cultivable area might be enormously extended if the water supply could be properly utilised by means of canals and reservoirs.

From the time of the Caliphs downwards this

truth seems to have been recognised by the more enlightened Egyptian sovereigns and statesmen. It was the Caliph Omar who gave the following advice to his viceroy: "Beware of money-lenders, and devote one-third of thy income to making canals." Had Ismail taken this counsel of perfection to heart, the regeneration of Egypt need not have been left to Great Britain and the other Great Powers.

Irrigation.—The irrigation question is therefore most important—in fact, the commercial and agricultural prosperity of Egypt is inseparably connected with the scientific disposal of the over-flowing waters of the Nile, and still more closely are the finances bound up with the great water question. This fact was recognised even by ancient Egyptian law, which regulated the land tax according to the water supply.

To understand, even in outline, the agriculture of Egypt, two great facts must be borne in mind. Firstly, the country is watered not by rain, but by the river. In Upper Egypt rain practically never falls, and even in Lower Egypt it is a *quantité negligeable.* Secondly, the river is not only the irrigator but the fertiliser of the soil.

Having grasped these essential facts, we are able to understand the reason of there being two systems of agriculture in Egypt. In Upper Egypt the natural inundation is not supplemented by a subsidiary system of irrigation canals, the aim of the cultivator being to cover as much land as possible with the Nile water and its deposit of fertilising mud. In the more scientific farming of the Delta, the efforts of the cultivation are mainly confined to controlling the Nile inundation, to keep it away during high flood, and to retain as much as possible of the water during the period of low Nile.

The English engineers, mostly trained in India, did not fall into the error of attempting to carry out the various undertakings connected with irrigation from the headquarters at Cairo. The country was divided into five circles of irrigation, of which four were entrusted to the new comers from India. This plan of localising the engineering talent proved a complete success.

A great impetus has also been given to the equally important work of extending the drainage system into the lower and more highly-cultivated tracts where water is abundant, and where the soil would in time deteriorate if drains were not constructed. Drainage in the Delta has also been put on a proper footing, and it has now a complete network of main and subsidiary canals designed on scientific principles.

3. Justice.—In the department of justice and police little progress has been made towards reform, and yet in no department is the principle of self-government more necessary. No effective interference took place till about 1889, which may account for the slow development in this branch of government.

The judicial system in Egypt is fourfold. (1) The old Koranic system worked by the *Mehkennehs* or Courts of the Religious Law, which are now mainly confined to dealing with the personal status of Mohammedans. (2) The mixed courts, which deal with civil actions between foreigners of different nationalities, or between natives and foreigners, and in small degree with the criminal offences of foreigners. (3) The system, or no system, of the consular courts, which deal with the crimes of foreigners. (4) Finally, there is the system of the new native courts, which deal with civil actions between natives or with crimes committed by natives. Of all these, it is only the native courts which the English have taken in hand, and that not till within the last few years.

These native courts are in one sense, though ranking only as Courts of First Instance, the most important of all as affecting the greatest number of people, but the English were at first chary of doing more than giving advice. The original *personnel* of the native court was very unsatisfactory, and jobbing and nepotism were rife. Sir J. Scott entered upon the delicate work of reform in a judicious and moderate spirit. He wisely contented himself with modifying the judicial system without radically altering the procedure and machinery of the law. Good authorities are of opinion that, taken collectively, the native tribunals give every sign of working admirably with a judicious leaven of European judges.

4. Police.—At present the police of each province are under the authority of the Mudir, but on the other hand his orders must be given to them through their own local officers. He has no power to interfere with the discipline and organisation of the force, nor can he make use of it except for the purposes of maintaining order and repressing crime.

In the Department of the Interior important reforms in the maintenance of public security have been effected in addition to the remodelled police, mainly since the establishment of a responsible English official, Sir. J. L. Gorst, who was appointed in 1894. He is the virtual head of this department, though the titular head is a native statesman. His chief work has been the reorganisation of the village watchmen (*Ghaffirs*), who serve as a supplementary police force. Thus a regular chain of authorities was effected in the machinery of government, by which the central authority in Cairo was in touch with the fellahs in the remotest district of the Upper Nile Valley.

5. Sanitation.—In the matter of sanitary reform,

the Egyptian Government has only recently awoke to its pressing need, and till recently this department remained in a most unsatisfactory state, which is probably due to the paucity of funds available. This is virtually admitted by Lord Cromer in his 1897 report:—

"It is only since 1894 that the Egyptian Government has been able to turn its attention seriously to those numerous reforms which involve increased expenditure on any considerable scale. Amongst the objects which most nearly concern the general welfare of Egypt, it cannot be doubted that the reconquest of some portion, at all events, of the Soudan, takes a very high place. It is to the accomplishment of this object that the attention of the Egyptian Government must, for the time being, be mainly directed.

"No Government, and certainly not the semi-internationalised Government of Egypt, can afford to embark at once and at the same moment in a number of expensive and difficult operations. I do not doubt that the day of the Egyptian sanitary reformer will come, but under the circumstances to which I alluded above, I fear, though I say it with regret, that some little while must yet elapse before the question of improved sanitation in Egypt can be taken seriously in hand."

Then a great deal must be allowed for the horribly

insanitary habits of the natives. Though personally clean, and not averse to the use of water, the huts of the fellaheen are indescribably filthy. Then again the religious prejudices of the people make the task of the sanitary reformer extremely difficult, for any injudicious interference might easily excite a fanatical opposition, which would stand in the way of reform. However, under the judicious management of Rogers Pasha, a large number of mosques, which were perfect centres of infection, have been placed in a proper sanitary condition.

Drainage of Cairo.—One of the most important measures in the matter of public health, which has lately received the attention of the Government, is the drainage of the capital. "This is a tremendous undertaking, estimated to cost at least £500,000. The necessity has long been recognised, but it has been put off from year to year, owing to want of money—not so much absolute want of money, as want of power to apply money that actually existed to the desired object, owing to the usual and ten-times-explained necessity of obtaining the consent of the Powers, or, more properly, the consent of France—for none of the others made any difficulty. France was finally appeased by the appointment of an International Commission to examine the various competing schemes." This Commission, composed of an Englishman, a Frenchman, and a German, sat in the winter of 1896-97, and ended by proposing a scheme of its own, for which preliminary plans are at present being made. "So in two or three years we may hope to see Cairo drained, in which case that city, or at any rate the European quarter of it, will very likely be one of the healthiest places of residence in the world."

6. **Education.**—Till recently the educational system seemed little affected by the pervading spirit of reform, but no department has borne richer fruit of late years.

The famous Azhar University, "a petrified University, which rests like a blight upon the religious and intellectual life of the country," has moulded all the religious training in Egypt, the result being that previous to 1884 the few Government schools had been boycotted by parents of the dominant faith; now, however, the better-class Mohammedans are beginning to tolerate the Government foundations, and the numbers are steadily increasing.

To come to a higher form of public education—the art of government. Little progress has been made in developing representative institutions in the machinery of government. There is, it is true, a Legislative Council, but this is not of great importance in the body politic. There is also the General

Assembly, which is simply the Council enlarged by a popular element. This has one important function, for no *new* taxes can be imposed without its consent. As, however, this Assembly only meets once every two years, it cannot play a considerable part in Egyptian politics. The time, in fact, has not yet come for applying the principle of representative government in any great degree to the national affairs of Egypt.

The above is a brief epitome of the development and results of the more important reforms in the administration of Egypt under British influence. For a good deal of the information embodied in this chapter I have laid under contribution an able study of Modern Egypt, *The Making of Egypt* (see "Bibliography"), by Sir Alfred Milner. Most of the quoted portions are also taken from this admirable and thoroughly well-informed work.

II.—RECENT ARCHÆOLOGICAL RESEARCH

The work of exploration in Egypt is chiefly undertaken by the Government Department of Antiquities and the Egypt Exploration Fund. The operations of this Society are characterised by great thoroughness and scientific zeal, and are conducted with a conscientiousness which is not always appreciated at its full value by the ordinary tourist, who is naturally inclined to give greater credit to the more practical and less scientific explorations of the Egyptian Government. But the aims of these two bodies are different. The Egypt Exploration Fund is a purely scientific society, while the Government Department chiefly devotes its attention to preserving and restoring the famous monuments and temples which attract the ordinary visitor.

Thebes.—During the last four winters the Exploration Fund have been carrying on extensive excavations at Thebes, with the view of thoroughly clearing out the wonderful temple of Queen Hatshepset at Dar-el-Bahari. This work is now finished, and every portion of this beautiful building can be seen by tourists.

Beni Hassan.—Another valuable work of the Egypt Exploration Fund within recent years has been the exhaustive archæological survey of the famous rock-tombs of Beni Hassan. The results of this stupendous undertaking, in which thousands of wall sculptures and inscriptions were transcribed and translated, supplemented by an enormous number of plans, diagrams, and "squeezes," are to be found in *Beni Hassan*, the *magnum opus* of the Society, consisting of four folio volumes.

Previous to 1883, when the Egypt Exploration Fund was founded, the historical value of many important discoveries had been considerably discounted, owing to the haphazard manner in which excavations and archæological researches had been undertaken, and this carelessness must be attributed to the insufficient supervision of the native diggers by the Museum authorities, who in most sites had the monopoly of digging. Within recent years, excavating has been carried on more intelligently, and with a greater appreciation of the value of full and accurate records of each object discovered, without which the most important discoveries, from the dealer's point of view, have little value in the eyes of scholars and archæologists.

Naukratis.—The discoveries at Naukratis, an ancient Greek settlement of the seventh century B.C., are of peculiar interest to art students. This ancient site is just beyond the native village of Nekrash, a few miles from Tel-el-Barud, a station on the Cairo and Alexandria Railway. Researches here have thrown considerable light on the life of the early Greek settlers who founded the city in the time of Psammetikhos, about 660 B.C. Professor Petrie brought away from the mounds of rubbish here a large collection of Greek vases and statuettes, many of which can now be seen in the British Museum.

Pithom.—Another important work by Professor Petrie, of peculiar interest to Biblical students, was the identification of the site of Pithom, the famous treasure city of the Pharaohs, in the mounds of Maskhuteh, a few miles west of Ismailia.

Equally sensational was the finding, by the same indefatigable explorer, of the Temple of Sneferu (the first king of the fourth dynasty), at the foot of the "False Pyramid" of Medum. An extraordinary circumstance in the discovery of this ancient temple was that it was found absolutely perfect, with even the roof entire, forty feet beneath the surface.

Tel-el-Amarna.—Tel-el-Amarna, some fifty miles north of Assiout, is the site of several interesting discoveries. The Great Temple of the "heretic king," Khu-en-Aten, was discovered by Lepsius, but systematically explored and described by Professor Petrie during the winter of 1891-92. Here were found the famous cuneiform tablets, which have added so much to our knowledge of Egypt's foreign relations during the reigns of the last kings of the eighteenth dynasty.

Side by side with the more scientific work of archæological research undertaken by the Egypt Exploration Fund, is the equally important, but more mechanical work of the Egyptian Government, which is mainly confined to the unearthing and clearing of rubbish the buried portions of the great monuments and temples of the Upper Nile, which may be considered as the great show-place for tourists.

Karnak.—At Karnak important work has been done. All the money raised by the Government tax levied on visitors to the ancient monuments during last winter (1896-97) was devoted to the restoration and excavation here. "Under the superintendence of M. de Morgan," says Lord Cromer in his last report, "great progress has been made during the last year in the work of preserving these temples. A large amount of earth, which filled the great courtyard and the Hall of Columns, has been removed; the bases of the columns have been cleared from contact with the salted earth and repaired with cement. The fallen stones have been numbered and collected, with a view possibly to their being replaced at some future time."

Island of Philæ.—During the past year Captain Lyons has been actively engaged in excavating likely sites in the Island of Philæ, and clearing the Temple of Isis of the debris of centuries, and the ruins of a Coptic village with which a portion of the building had been covered. In the course of the excavation of likely sites, several small temples were discovered. Although this archæological work was merely supplementary to the great engineering work undertaken by the Government, of forming a huge dam at this part of the river, it was carried out most thoroughly and efficiently. Indirectly, then, the Assouan Reservoir Scheme, which was so strenuously opposed by archæologists and artists, has been the means of promoting antiquarian research in Philæ.

The Pyramids.—In the Ghizeh Pyramid Plateau we reach a site known to every tourist. Unfortunately this district, although of the highest archæological interest, has never been properly worked, owing to the Government digging monopoly. At the Pyramid of Dahshur, however, at the southern end of this extensive necropolis, much has been done by M. de Morgan, the new Director of the Museum, and his thorough researches have resulted in a most valuable mine of tombs being brought to light. The magnificent sets of jewellery found here, now in the Cairo Museum, are familiar to every traveller in Egypt. "The exquisite delicacy, skill, and taste of this work surpasses all that is yet known. The pectorals are formed by soldering walls of gold on to a base plate, which is elaborately chased with details on the back. Between these walls or ribs of gold are inserted minutely cut stones—cornelian, lazuli, and felspar—to give the vari-coloured design. In this, and in the beads of gold, the astounding minuteness of the work and perfect delicacy of execution exceed the limits of mere naked-eye inspection."

Oxyrhynchus.—The season of 1896-97 was noteworthy for the discovery of some of the most valuable discoveries of papyri in the whole history of Egyptian exploration. This includes the famous "Logia"—a second-century papyrus containing some remarkable sayings of Our Lord, a third-century copy of the first chapter of St. Matthew—a *century older* than the oldest MSS. of the New Testament, and a long fragment of the fourth book of Thucydides (chapters 36-41).

These extraordinary discoveries, which can only be compared in point of interest to the sensational find of the mummies of the Pharaohs at Thebes in

1881, are due to the enterprise and skill of Messrs. Grenfell and Hunt of Oxford University. The place of discovery was Behneseh, which occupies the site of the Roman town of Oxyrhynchus, on the edge of the Libyan Desert, 120 miles south of Cairo and some 8 miles west of the Nile. The best specimens of this wonderful find were claimed by the authorities of the Ghizeh Museum, but the rest of the collection was despatched to England. The papyri consist of some 2300 pieces, from the first to the tenth century, and comprise, in short, in addition to the purely literary fragments and texts, "specimens of almost everything committed to writing, from an imperial edict to the private memoranda of a fellah."

The Logia.—This document has aroused a considerable amount of interest among theological students, and has given rise to many problems. Some critics consider that this papyrus is a fragment of the well-known, but of course non-canonical, "Gospel according to the Egyptians." A more satisfactory view, though not free from difficulties, is that this papyrus is what it professes to be, a collection of some of Our Lord's sayings. "These, judging from their archaic tone and framework, were put together not later than the end of the first, or the beginning of the second century, and it is quite possible that they embody a tradition independent of those which have taken shape in our canonical Gospels."

Deshâsheh.—This part of the Libyan Desert has proved a prolific field to explorers, as, only forty miles north of Behneseh, Professor Petrie, early in 1897, found at Deshâsheh (a few miles south of Beni Suef, but on the other side of the river) a number of fifth-dynasty tombs. The principal results obtained were several statues of Prince Nenkheftka (about 3500 B.C.). One of these figures, which are remarkably artistic productions, has been brought to England.

The skeletons found in the tombs are of the greatest interest to historical and anthropological students. Most of these had evidently been carefully dissected and put together again. This, in the opinion of Professor Petrie, points to an unusual method of burial anterior to the age of mummies, and suggests a cannibal ancestry. This theory is ventilated in a striking article by the Professor in the *Contemporary*, June 1897.

The above is, of course, the merest outline of the more important results in the last few years in the wide field of Egyptian exploration.

III.—BIBLIOGRAPHY OF RECENT POPULAR WORKS ON EGYPT

The following list includes the principal popular Books of Travel in Egypt published within the last few years. A few of the standard works of reference are also included :—

ADAMS, FRANCIS.—*The New Egypt.* 5s. 1893. (Unwin.)

ARNOLD, J. T. B.—*Palms and Temples.* Notes of a Dahabeah Voyage. 12s.

BAEDEKER.—*Lower Egypt.* 16s. 1895. (Dulau.) Baedeker gives more information about Cairo and its environs (about 180 pages) than Murray, but the latter (last ed. 1896) is more up to date.

—— *Upper Egypt.* 10s. 1892. (Dulau.) A new edition of Baedeker's *Upper Egypt* will be published in the winter of 1897-98. Indispensable for students.

BARBIER, J.—*Handbook for Cairo.* (French.) 5 frs.

BELL, C. F. MOBERLEY.—*From Pharaoh to Fellah.* 16s. 1889. (Wells, Gardner, and Co.)

—— *Khedives and Pashas.* 10s. (Sampson Low.) An admirable sketch of contemporary Egyptian statesmen. Should be read in conjunction with Sir Alfred Milner's *England in Egypt.*

BELL, Rev. C. D., D.D.—*A Winter on the Nile.* 6s. (Hodder.)

BENTLEY, A. J. M., M.D., and Rev. C. G. GRIFFENHOOFE, M.A.—*Wintering in Egypt.* 3s. 6d. 2nd Ed. 1896. (Simpkin, Marshall, and Co.)

BIRDWOOD, SIR F.—*Travels in the East of the Czarewitch (Nicholas II.)* 1896. (Constable.)

BOURQUET, A.—*The Story of France and England in Egypt.* (French). 1897. (Nourrit et Cie.)

BRADSHAW. — *Handbook for India, Turkey, and Egypt.* 5s.

BRUGSCH BEY.—*Egypt under the Pharaohs.* 3rd Ed. 18s. (Murray.)

BUDGE, E. A. WALLIS, M.A.—*Dwellers on the Nile.*

—— *The Nile: Notes for Travellers in Egypt.* 4th Ed. 1895. (Cook and Son.) This useful work of reference is not for sale, but is written solely for Egyptian tourists travelling under Messrs. Cook's arrangements.

BUTCHER, E. L.—*The Story of the Church of Egypt.* 2 vols. 16s. 1897. (Smith, Elder, and Co.)

BUTLER, A. J.—*Court Life in Egypt.* 2nd Ed. 12s. (Chapman.)

—— *Ancient Coptic Churches.* 2 vols. 1884.

CANNEY, H. E. LEIGH, M.D.—*The Meteorology of Egypt and its Influence on Disease.* 1897. (Ballière.) The best book published on the climate of the Upper Nile.

CASSELL AND CO.—*The Picturesque Mediterranean.* 2 Vols. £4 : 4s. 1891. The Chapter on Egypt by E. A. Reynolds-Ball.

COOK'S *Handbook for Egypt.* With Maps, 359 pp. 6s. 1897. (Thomas Cook and Son.) Admirably compiled.

COOKE, E. W.—*Leaves from my Sketch-book.* (Murray.)

CURTIS.—*Nile Notes of a Howadji.*

CURZON.—*Monasteries of the Levant.* Cheap Ed. 1s. 1897. (G. Newnes.)

EBERS, G.—*Egypt: Descriptive, Historical, and Picturesque.* Translated by Clara Bell. 2 Vols. 42s. 1887. (Cassell and Co., Limited.) Considered a classic, and many modern travel-writers have laid this encyclopædic work under contribution.

EDEN.—*The Nile without a Dragoman.* 1871.

EDINBURGH REVIEW.—*The Plain of Thebes.* October 1897.

EDWARDS, A. B.—*Pharaohs, Fellahs and Explorers.* New Ed. 18s. 1893. (Osgood.) This book, which is unfortunately handicapped by its *ad captandum* title, is a most exhaustive and conscientious work, and, although written many years ago, it holds its own as the best popular introduction to Egyptology.

EDWARDS, A. B.—*A Thousand Miles up the Nile.* 3rd Ed. 7s. 6d. (Routledge.) This book is perhaps one of the best works on Egyptian travel ever written.

GAUTIER, TH.—*L'Orient.*

GORDON, LADY DUFF.—*Last Letters from Egypt.* An admirable series of letters describing Luxor before it became a fashionable winter resort. 9s. 2nd Ed. (Macmillan.)

GREEN, S. E.—*Pictures from Bible Lands.*

HOGARTH, D. G.—*A Wandering Scholar in the Levant.* 2nd Ed. 1897. 7s. 6d. (Murray.)

HOPLEY.—*Under Egyptian Palms.*

HOSKINS.—*A Winter in Upper and Lower Egypt.*

JOANNE.—*Egypte.* 30 fr. (Hachette.) The best French guide-book on Egypt published.

KINGLAKE, A. W.—*Eothen.* 1s. Pop. Ed. 1897. (Blackwood.)

LANE, E. W.—*Modern Egyptians.* Pop. Ed. 3s. 6d. (Ward, Lock.)

LANE-POOLE, STANLEY.—*Egypt.* 3s. 6d. (S. Low and Co.)

—— *Social Life in Egypt.* 1883. 21s. (Virtue.)

—— *Cairo: Sketches of its History and Social Life.* 2nd Ed. 1892. (Virtue.)

—— *Cairo Fifty Years Ago.* New Ed. 1896. (Murray.)

—— *Studies in a Mosque.* 2nd Ed. 1892. (Allen.)

—— *Art of the Saracens in Egypt.* 1886. (Chapman and Hall.)

LEFÉBRE.—*La Vallée du Nil.*

LELAND.—*Egyptian Sketch-book.* 1873.

LOFTIE, Rev. W. J.—*A Ride in Egypt from Assiout to Luxor.* 1879.

—— *Orient Line Guide.* 5th Ed. 1894. 2s. 6d. (S. Low.)

LUNN, Rev. H. S., M.D.—*How to Visit the Mediterranean.* 10s. 1896. (Horace Marshall.) contains articles on Alexandria and Cairo by E. A. Reynolds-Ball.

LYNCH, J.—*Egyptian Sketches.* 1890.

MACGREGOR, J.—*Rob Roy on the Nile and Jordan.* 7s. 6d. 1871. (Murray.)

MADDEN, J. M., M.D.—*Health Resorts in Europe and Africa.* 3s. 6d. 1888. (Sonnenschein.)

MAHAFFY, Prof. J.P.—*The Empire of the Ptolemies.* 1895. (Macmillan.)

MANNING, Rev. SAMUEL, D.D.—*The Land of the Pharaohs.* New Ed. 1897. 8s. (Religious Tract Society.)

MARTINEAU, HARRIET.—*Eastern Life.*

MARIETTE PASHA.—*Outlines of Ancient Egyptian History.* Edited by M. Brodrick. 5s. (Murray.)

—— *Monuments of Upper Egypt.* 6s. (Kegan Paul.)

MASPERO, Prof.—*Egyptian Archæology.* Translated by A. B. Edwards. 2nd Ed. 10s. 6d.

—— *The Dawn of Civilisation.* £2 : 5s. 1896. (S. P. C. K.)

—— *The Struggle of the Nations.* £1 : 8s. 1896. (S. P. C. K.)

MAY, W. PAGE, M.D.—*Helouan and its Waters.* 1897. (John Bale and Sons.)

M'COAN, J. C.—*Egypt under Ismail.* 7s. 6d. (Chapman.)

MERIWETHER, L.—*Afloat and Ashore on the Mediterranean.* New Ed. 6s. 1891. (S. Low.)

MILNER, SIR A.—*England in Egypt.* 7s. 6d. 2nd Ed. 1893. (Arnold.) Deservedly ranks as a classic.

MONCRIEFF, A. R. HOPE.—*Where to go Abroad.* 3s. 6d. 1893. (A. and C. Black.)

MONTBARD, G.—*The Land of the Sphinx.* 16s. 1894. (Hutchinson.)

MUIR, Sir W.—*The Mamelukes.* 10s. 6d. 1896. (Smith, Elder, and Co.)

MURRAY, JOHN.—*Handbook for Egypt.* 15s. 9th Ed. 1896. (Murray.) This edition has been rewritten, and is admirably edited by Miss M. Brodrick, Ph.D.

OXLEY, J. M.—*Egypt and the Wonders of the Land of the Pharaohs.* 1884. 7s. 6d. (Hodder.)

PARSONS, A. R.—*New Light from the Pyramid.* 1893. A fanciful metaphysical speculation on the origin of the Pyramids.

PETRIE, W. M. FLINDERS.—*History of Egypt.* Six vols. 6s. each. (Methuen.) In preparation. Will be probably finished in the course of 1898.

PETRIE, W. M. FLINDERS.—*Ten Years' Digging in Egypt: 1881-1891.* 6s. (R. T. S.).

—— *The Great Pyramid.* 1888. The best scientific description yet published.

PLUNKETT, Major R. E.—*Walks in Cairo.* 2s. 1889. A slight but well-written brochure dealing with the Mosques and Bazaars. (Simpkin, Marshall, and Co.)

POLLARD, JOSEPH.—*The Land of the Monuments.* 7s. 6d. 1896. (Hodder and Stoughton.)

POOLE, R. S.—*The Cities of Egypt.* 5s. (Smith, Elder, and Co.)

RAE, W. FRASER.—*Egypt To-Day.* 16s. 1892. (Bentley.)

RAWNSLEY, H. D., M.A.—*Notes for the Nile.* 5s. (Heinemann.)

REYNOLDS-BALL, E. A.—*Mediterranean Winter Resorts.* 414 pages. 3rd Ed. 5s. (Kegan Paul.) Gives 33 pages of information on Cairo, intended mainly for invalid visitors. A new edition, 500 pages, price 6s., will be published in October 1898.

—— *The City of the Caliphs.* 380 pages. 12s. 6d. nett. 1897. (Estes and Lauriat: Boston, U.S.A.) This gives a description of Cairo and its principal sights and excursions, and of the Nile and its antiquities.

RITCHIE, J. EWING.—*Cities of the Dawn.* 1897. 5s. (Fisher Unwin.) A very readable book of travel.

RUSSELL, R. H.—*On the Edge of the Orient.* 1897. (Kegan Paul.)

SANDWITH, F. M., M.D.—*Egypt as a Winter Resort.* 3s. 6d. 1889. (Kegan Paul.) Of great value to invalids.

SAYCE, Prof. A. H.—*The Egypt of the Hebrews.* 2nd Ed. 1897. 7s. 6d. (Rivingtons.)

SCHAFF, P., D.D.—*Through Bible Lands.* 3s. 6d. (Nisbet.)

SHELLEY, Capt.—*The Birds of Egypt.* 1872.

SLATIN PASHA.—*Fire and Sword in the Soudan.* Trans. by Lieut.-Col. WINGATE. New Ed. 1897. 6s. (Arnold.)

SMITH, G. BARNETT.—*Life of Ferdinand de Lesseps.* 7s. 6d. 1895. (Allen.) A useful history of the Suez Canal is embodied in this biography.

STANLEY, H. M.—*Early Travels.* Vol. II. 1896. (S. Low.)

STUART, H. VILLIERS.—*Nile Gleanings.* 31s. 6d. 1880.

—— *Egypt after the War.* 1883.

TAYLOR, Canon ISAAC.—*Leaves from an Egyptian Note-Book.* 5s. 1888. (Kegan Paul.)

TIRARD, H. M.—*Sketches from a Nile Steamer.* 6s. 1891. (Kegan Paul.)

TRAILL, H. D.—*From Cairo to the Soudan Frontier.* 5s. 1896. (Lane.) Narrative of a Nile Trip in the Winter of 1895-96. One of the best books on the Nile voyage.

—— (Editor)—*The Capitals of the World.* 2 Vols. 63s. (Sampson Low.)

—— *Life of Lord Cromer.* 15s. 1897. (Bliss and Sands.)

VINCENT, FRANK.—*Actual Africa.* 1895.

WARBURTON, ELIAS.—*The Crescent and the Cross.* Cheap Ed. 6d. (Ward, Lock.) This famous record of travel, though describing Egypt under Mehemet Ali, will be found of great value by the nineteenth-century tourist.

WARNER, C. DUDLEY.—*My Winter on the Nile.* New Ed. 1881. 8s. (Houghton, Boston.)

WERNER, CARL.—*Nile Sketches.* 1871. (Sampson Low.)

WHATELEY, M. L.—*Scenes from Life in Cairo.* (R. T. S.)

WHITEHOUSE, F. COPE.—*How to save Egypt.* 1893. A plea for the Fayyoum Reservoir Scheme.

WHYLIE, J. A., LL.D.—*Egypt and its Future.*

WILKINS, ANTHONY.—*On the Nile with a Camera.* £1 : 1s. 1896. (Fisher Unwin.) Beautifully illustrated.

WILKINSON, Sir GARDNER.—*Ancient Egyptians.* 12s. New Edition, abridged. Two Vols. (Murray.)

WILSON, Sir ERASMUS.—*Cleopatra's Needle, with Notes on Egyptian Obelisks.* 1877.

WITHERBY, H. F.—*Light from the Land of the Sphinx.* 1896. (Stock.)

WOOD, H. F.—*The English in Egypt.* 1896. A slight but readable summary of the results of the English "veiled Protectorate."

ZINCKE, Rev. B.—*Egypt of the Pharaohs and the Khedives.* 1873.

An exhaustive bibliography of Egyptian literature up to 1885 has been published by Prince Ibrahim Hilmy, uncle of the Khedive. (2 Vols. 1887.)

INDEX

THE END

Printed by R. & R. CLARK, LIMITED, *Edinburgh*

BOOKS OF TRAVEL.

THROUGH FINLAND IN CARTS. By Mrs. ALEC TWEEDIE, Author of "A Girl's Ride in Iceland," "A Winter Jaunt to Norway," etc. With Map and 18 Full-page Illustrations. Demy 8vo., Cloth, Price 15s.

"From first to last there is not a dull page in the volume, which is admirably written, well illustrated, and full of humour. It is one of the best books of travel we have read for many a year."—*Illustrated Sporting and Dramatic News.* (The book of the week.)

NAPLES IN THE NINETIES. A Sequel to Naples in 1888. By E. NEVILLE ROLFE, H.B.M. Consul at Naples. With 18 Full-page Illustrations and 8 inserted in the Text. Crown 8vo, Cloth, Price 7s. 6d.

"People in search of a brightly-written, unconventional holiday handbook to Naples past and present could scarcely do better than procure Mr. Neville Rolfe's fascinating volume."—*Speaker.*

IN NORTHERN SPAIN. By Dr. HANS GADOW, M.A., Ph.D., F.R.S. Containing Map and 89 Illustrations. Demy 8vo, Cloth, Price 21s.

"Some years back 'Wild Spain,' one of the best books of its kind, made you desirous of knowing more of the country. And Hans Gadow has deepened this feeling in his excellent volume 'In Northern Spain,' and that to an enormous extent. Dwelling at inn or farm, or in their own tent, they saw the country as it has been seen but rarely, and they came to know the inhabitants as they can be known in no other fashion."—*Black and White.*

BRITTANY FOR BRITONS. The newest practical information about the Towns frequented by the English on the Gulf of St. Malo. By DOUGLAS SLADEN, Author of "A Japanese Marriage." Illustrated, Crown 8vo., Cloth, Price 2s. 6d.

"It is an inviting sketch of pleasant places possessing the charm of novelty without the drawback of remoteness, up to date, practical."—*Daily Telegraph.*

A. & C. BLACK, SOHO SQUARE, LONDON.

www.ingramcontent.com/pod-product-compliance
Lightning Source LLC
Chambersburg PA
CBHW021059030726
47496CB00006B/1917
9783337177935